In this WMG Writer's Guide, award-winning author Kristine Kathryn Rusch offers words of wisdom for writers who suffer from chronic illnesses and who want to keep working, to improve their craft and spread their creative wings.

WMG WRITER'S GUIDE SERIES

Writing a Novel in Five Days While Traveling

The Magic Bakery: Copyright in the Modern World of Fiction Publishing

Closing the Deal on Your Terms: Agents, Contracts and Other Considerations

Writing a Novel in Seven Days: A Hands-on Example

Heinlein's Rules: Five Simple Business Rules for Writing

How to Write Fiction Sales Copy

Stages of a Fiction Writer: Know Where You Stand on the Path to Writing

Writing into the Dark: How to Write aNovel Without an Outline

How to Write a Novel in Ten Days

Killing the Top Ten Sacred Cows of Publishing

Killing the Top Ten Sacred Cows of Indie Publishing

Surviving the Transition: How Writers Can Thrive in the New World of Publishing

The Pursuit of Perfection: And How It Harms Writers

The Write Attitude

Discoverability

Creating Your Author Brand

WRITING WITH CHRONIC ILLNESS

A WMG WRITER'S GUIDE

KRISTINE KATHRYN RUSCH

Writing with Chronic Illness
Copyright © 2019 by Kristine Kathryn Rusch
First published in 2018 in a slightly different version on kristinekathrynrusch.com
Published by WMG Publishing
Cover, layout, and design © copyright 2019 WMG Publishing
ISBN-13: 978-1-56146-081-6
ISBN-10: 1-56146-081-8

This book is licensed for your personal enjoyment only. All rights reserved.
This book, or parts thereof, may not be reproduced in any form without permission.

WRITING WITH CHRONIC ILLNESS

CONTENTS

Introduction	xiii

MY PERSONAL JOURNEY

The Structure of This Section	3
Health History: A Short Report	5
Best-Laid Plans of Mice and Kittens	17
Settling In: (A Process Blog)	21
Schedules and Structure	29
Thriving Despite…	35

THE GENERAL USEFUL STUFF

The Structure of This Section	41
Priorities	43
Productivity	53
Discipline	63
Calling in Sick	79
Healthy Time Off	85
Comparisons	89
The Point	95

About the Author	101

For Dean
You have my undying gratitude for all you've done

INTRODUCTION

I used to hide the fact that I had chronic health problems. When I was in my twenties and sick at least five days a month, I figured that was life. Everyone had health problems that knocked them on their ass at least one day per week, right?

I was raised by a difficult mother who had chronic health issues of her own, and who was, by the time I was old enough to pay attention, a full-blown alcoholic. My father, a functioning alcoholic, was never sick a day in his life—or at least, he never missed work. At his job, he accumulated sick days which never expired, and that gave him years of back pay when he retired.

My mother treated his good health like a fluke, and I took that in. Good health was unusual; bad health was the norm.

My health started to crater in my teens, after a very serious bout of mononucleosis. I was sick for six weeks and never quite the same after that. I'm not sure if it was a confluence of factors or if that illness did play havoc with my immune system. I've never asked a doctor about either possibility. I do know that going on the birth control pill in 1979 strongly exacerbated all of my health issues. I was nineteen. My migraines increased dramatically. I nearly walked into a zooming ambulance one afternoon because I was so zoned out with a headache that I didn't hear the siren or see the flashing lights.

The best doctor I ever had told me, in the 1990s, that the super strong pill of the 1970s destroyed the health of many women, most of whom had to go on disability because they couldn't work.

I get that. It would have been a struggle for me to hold a full-time job—the kind you had to go to every day and be present for—from my mid-thirties onward. By that point, I was down with a migraine or other health issues for twenty-one out of twenty-eight days. I learned to grade the migraines by severity. The severity levels had nothing to do with the real world and everything to do with me. Judging severity went like this:

Can I write? Yes/No
If yes, can I write fiction?
If no, can I write nonfiction?
If still no, can I read?
If still no, will a nap cure it?
If still no, take the damn day off and watch TV and hope the migraine goes away on its own.

Migraines were my body's way of shutting me down. I have a host of allergies, from serious fragrance allergies to food allergies that can make me seriously ill for days. I'm pretty sure the fragrance allergies are related to the chemicals used to make fragrances here in the United States; when I traveled through France and found myself trapped in duty-free areas reeking of perfume, I never had more than a case of sniffles. France heavily regulates its perfume industry, requiring natural ingredients.

Introduction

I have learned, since I moved to Las Vegas, that I can sit in restaurants near all-natural perfume shops, but can't walk past the cleaning aisle in the grocery store. The cleaning aisle is filled with chemicals; the all-natural perfume shops are not.

But you didn't pick up this book to hear about my health problems. You picked this up because you're suffering from problems of your own, or you have friends or family members who suffer, and who also want to write.

I've managed a heck of a writing career while sick for days on end. I also managed to edit nearly full time in my thirties because I didn't have to go to an office, and because I could take a nap when my body required one. I also didn't have to drive anywhere. One of the severity tests I gave myself was about driving—was I alert enough to be behind the wheel? Often, with my migraines, the answer is no.

I never told the publisher I worked for in my thirties that I had health issues. He was across the country, and didn't see me daily (or he would have known). My friends knew that I couldn't come to dinner at certain places because those restaurants would cross contaminate the food or that I had to flee some buildings when a person wearing too much cologne entered. It seemed, from the outside, like I was an oversensitive creature who couldn't handle the real world.

Or maybe that's my insecurities talking.

Because I made a point of getting my work done and done well. I worked to deadline and never missed due to health. I was reliable, hard-working, and good at what I did.

But what I did was never in person.

In person created problems. As my career flourished and I had to travel to conventions and meetings with editors, the health problems showed up. Airline travel has always been a nightmare for me; hotels are worse. (I spent one night in Germany sniffing pillows with a hotel concierge. Seriously. He and I were looking for one that didn't stink of someone's cologne, so I had something to rest my head on that night. I finally opted for some bundled up clothing from my suitcase. The next morning, the hotel gave me a brand new pillow out of the bag.)

I had to stop doing one-on-one sessions or coffee dates with fans or wannabe writers because I couldn't guarantee that I could concentrate on them. I gave talks that I considered plug-and-play: I could recite the words even if I was so sick I could barely handle the light.

But as time went on, I found myself canceling more and more appearances that I had already agreed to. I finally had to cut back on everything that was happening in person. I couldn't guarantee that I would be able to speak coherently or hold down my breakfast or stay out of the emergency room.

It became impossible to hide my health concerns in public, so I became a recluse. I talked about health issues on my nonfiction blog, which I have written consistently since 2009 (with a short hiatus to finish a large project—the hiatus, I now realize, due more to my bad health and inability to concentrate than the project itself). I would mention that I have health problems and if you scroll back through ten years of blog posts, you'll find a few of them that start with "My chronic health issue raised its ugly head this week..." but I'd rarely go into more detail than that.

Some of my reticence comes from the fact that I began my working life in the 1970s, when the laws were different. You could be fired if you had too many health problems back then. I also had the hard-working example of my never-ill father. People who worked didn't get sick. Period. End of story.

I worked. Therefore, I didn't get sick. Even though I often was.

Getting sick regularly also seemed like weakness to me. I'd

Introduction

rather see myself (then and now) as someone strong and healthy than as a sickly woman who could barely make it out of bed some days. A friend of mine and I actually had T-shirts made that labeled us reluctant delicate flowers, because we both struggled against the negative self-image that comes from constantly dealing with bad health.

I'm better now, but the health problems remain. Some of the improvement comes with age—many of my health issues in my thirties and forties came from hormonal issues—and some of the improvement comes because I have figured out how to manage the chronic health problems. A great deal of the improvement came when I moved from Oregon to Nevada. In Las Vegas, where I live now, airflow is better, there are no mold issues, and most of the buildings are new so they don't leak chemicals. Here in the desert, the air is dry so it doesn't hold fragrance. Restaurants, used to tourists and terrified of a bad online review, cater to my food allergies, and grocery stores actually have items I can eat and cook (unlike Oregon, which is still [mostly] stuck in the 1950s when it comes to healthy foods).

Eating right and breathing clean air make a huge difference. That, plus the behaviors I adopted when I was in Oregon, have made me a much healthier version of the woman I was. Which is startling, because there are lifestyle adjustments that come with getting healthier that I did not expect, things that I will discuss later in the book.

When I told Allyson Longueira of WMG Publishing that I was compiling this book from my blog posts, I had thought that there were more posts about chronic health problems than there were. I thought I had been shouting about my bad health from the rooftops. Instead, I would mention the issue in passing and write about the solutions.

The mentions in passing made me realize just how much

Introduction

I've downplayed the illness side of my life, not just on the blogs, but in general. Tough it out, make it through, and never let them see you sweat.

I prefer being that woman. But I have a lot to share when it comes to living with and writing while suffering from chronic illness.

So I've put together this book partly from old blog posts, and with more new material than I expected.

I also decided to divide the book into two parts.

One part will deal with my personal journey. I don't think it's fair to talk about chronic illness without revealing some of what I'm dealing with on a regular basis. I know many of you want to read about that.

I also know that many of you don't care about what I'm dealing with at all. You just want to know what my tricks are for getting through the day.

Those of you who don't want the personal side should skip ahead to the section titled "The General Useful Stuff." The chapters in there will show you the structures I imposed (and still impose) on my day and life in order to get as much done as I have.

If you are suffering from debilitating health conditions, you have my heartfelt sympathy. I hope this book can help you. If you bought this book for a friend or loved one, thank you for recognizing what they're struggling with. A journey through bad health is always easier when someone sees what you're going through, even if they can't fix it.

I hope this book provides a few solutions for you. If nothing else, I hope it helps you realize that you're not alone. We all have issues and, I'm slowly realizing, it is easier when we discuss them with each other. That way we don't reinvent the wheel. We can build on what others have learned.

Introduction

I hope you can build on what I have learned. And I wish you all the best.

—Kristine Kathryn Rusch
Las Vegas, Nevada
February 13, 2019

MY PERSONAL JOURNEY

THE STRUCTURE OF THIS SECTION

As I wrote in the introduction, I write a weekly business blog. I often repurpose the blog posts into nonfiction books, which is what I thought I would do here. Imagine my surprise when I realized that so many of the "in-depth" posts were simply a passing mention.

Still, there are posts about my health that I can share here. They don't entirely make sense out of context, which I will give you in the next chapter.

That chapter, "Health History: A Short Report," discusses what I've been through, but not in great detail. I'm still that reticent woman who really would prefer to discuss anything but my health. I don't want to minimize, though. My life was (and still is in many ways) restricted by my health.

So, for context, I'll give you as much as I'm comfortable with.

My move to Las Vegas in 2018 was transformative. I have finally found an environment I can thrive in. The move was sudden: we had to get me out of Oregon, and the toxic living situation I was in, in the space of two months. Most of that burden fell on my husband Dean, who is an absolute rock.

In addition to being transformative, though, the move was disruptive. I had to learn new ways of being and how to manage my day-to-day life. I'm writing this in February of 2019, nearly a year after the move, and I'm still managing the disruption.

The best way to handle chronic health problems is a set structure, and I blew that structure up in 2018. I'll be dealing with some of that in the next section, but I'm sharing the blog posts here about the disruption, so that you can see how it all worked for me in what was real time. All of the chapters in this section will have the date they were written (or completed) up front.

Finally, this section ends with a guest blog I wrote on writing with chronic health issues. I wrote that post in August of 2018.

I'm sure you'll find tidbits here that can help you on your journey. But mostly, this is just background so that you can figure out where I'm coming from and how similar—or different—my struggle is from yours.

Again, if you want practical information only, skip this section and move to the next one.

Okay. Here we go.

HEALTH HISTORY: A SHORT REPORT
WRITTEN ON FEBRUARY 14, 2019

I suppose it's appropriate that I am writing this chapter on a soggy, rainy day in Las Vegas. I moved here eleven months ago, almost to the day, and have endured about five rainy days since. The constant sunlight has been a gift that I hadn't known I needed.

But this day, with its heavy rain, made me wake to darkness, replicating my old life on the Oregon Coast. I was off-balance, quite sad, and a little angry when I got up. I also felt trapped. I'll be heading to lunch soon in a favorite restaurant where I will write more on this book, partly to remind myself that I can eat well here, that I can go to normal places, and live a normal life. I am not trapped.

I *was* in Oregon. I will get to that in a moment. But I promised you a short history, and I have to tell you, writing this part is hard for me. I generally don't discuss my health with anyone except my husband, a few friends, and my doctors.

The Beginning

The first time I remember being sick—long-term, scary sick—was when I was sixteen. I contracted mononucleosis at the same time our high school teachers went on strike. We kids were protesting the strike, trying to get the teachers and the school board to talk. So in early January of 1977, we were staying up late, making posters, protesting in the snow and bitter cold, and generally being kids.

I went out with a boy I had a crush on to a late movie one night. He dropped me at home about one in the morning.

The next day, I couldn't talk. I had a fever of 104, and I had never been sicker. Apparently, I turned yellow, which scared the crap out of my mom. She drove me to the doctor who did something and prescribed something and came up with a diagnosis, and all I remember about any of that was feeling woozy and being unable to do much more than lie on the couch.

I read *The Lord of The Rings* trilogy during that illness, and thought I had hallucinated all of the details. It wasn't until the films came out that I realized, no, I got the details just fine. And they embedded in my dreams.

My illness coincided with the teacher's strike. I did not miss a single day of school because school had been canceled. I returned the same day as my friends, many of whom had no idea I had been sick until they saw me. I had lost twenty pounds while I was sick, which made me skeletal. I did not gain most of that weight back until the Freshman 15 in college.

I have no idea if mono broke my health or if my hormonal issues became serious at the same time. I do know that I saw myself as fragile from that point forward, never wanting to be that sick again in my life.

I really wasn't as sick as I would become later. I did a lot of things, traveled a lot (missing most of my senior year to senior trips), and have no real memory of being ill. I did seem to get a lot of food-borne illness, but teenage me often solved that by skipping meals.

I got sick more often after the bout of mono, but not enough to interfere with my life.

The interference started after I started the birth control pill in 1979. The pill then had 3% to 7% more estrogen than pills developed in the 1980s, and according to my doc in the 1990s, 10%-50% stronger than the pills issued then.

One article I just looked up said that the strong pills created a lot of adverse health effects. Um, yeah. In a lot of women. Including me.

I started the pill in June before my marriage in August. I was sick that entire summer. My family doctor kept adjusting the dose but I had days when I could barely function. Finally, after six months, I gave up. I stopped taking the pill and went back to other forms of contraception.

But the damage was done. My hormones were out of whack and remained that way for years. I got migraines whenever I had a hormonal change. I didn't know that, though, until I married Dean and he kept track. We could chart the appearance of those headaches to the day and hour. Then he informed the Best Doctor In The World (I still miss her), and she figured out the cause of those headaches.

She prescribed…birth control pills. And oh, my, God did we have a fight. She explained the history of the pill, showed me the science, and I agreed to try the extremely low-dose pill to regulate my hormones for a month or two.

Well, my hormonal migraines vanished. I went from being ill almost every day to only about 10 days out of 30. That was a great shift, which lasted until I had to be removed from the pill due to the dangers associated with my age.

And oh, was I mad about that.

Anyway.

One Giant Headache

By the 1990s, my life had become one gigantic headache. If I wasn't suffering from hormonal migraines, I was suffering from migraines triggered by my allergies. I have a wide variety of allergies. Studies say that kids who were raised in a pristine and extremely clean environment don't have time to develop immunities to dirt.

My mother, in addition to her other problems, was phobic about dirt. I have a vivid memory of being three, falling and nearly drowning in a pool of dirty water at a construction site behind our house. I managed to pull myself out of the water (fortunately, I knew how to swim), and arrived home, covered in mud. My mother was furious. She made me undress in the garage and walk across towels to the bathroom to get cleaned up—after she spanked me for getting so dirty. I don't think I ever told her where I got into the mud or how I had nearly drowned.

Mother cleaned everything, sometimes more than once. No clutter existed on tabletops, and if my father hadn't vetoed it strongly (I remember this too), we would have had plastic on the furniture. We had dogs, because my father liked them, but that was the extent of mess in our place. And the dog hair got vacuumed up every single day.

Anyway, that may have been the trigger for some of my allergies. I have always been allergic to perfumes and fragrances, but in my childhood most were made of natural ingredients. With the arrival of cheap perfumes and colognes (like Hai Karate), my allergies got worse. I couldn't walk past a perfume store in my early twenties without getting...you guessed it...a migraine.

Add to that food allergies that I had no idea I had (more below), and I would get all kinds of fun problems with the migraines—most of which either put me in a bathroom for hours or flat on my back with nausea.

I did not drink, though. I was sick enough. I blamed my alcoholic parents, mostly, but some of it was pretty simple. I couldn't imagine drinking to excess—which made people sick —when I had so few days of wellness as it was.

I read a lot, though, and learned about migraines. I learned to avoid my triggers—from cigarette smoke to perfumes and colognes to changes in air pressure to changes in sleep habits— and mostly managed to minimize the severity of the migraines, if not prevent some. But a lot of the headaches remained a mystery until my forties.

It wasn't until I moved to the Oregon Coast that I realized I was deeply horribly and awfully allergic to seafood. I didn't like it and rarely ate it, but when I did, I got sick. Midwestern girl that I was, I figured that I always got the bad shrimp or the just-turned oyster. Nope. What I thought was food poisoning (with all of its charms) was a severe allergic reaction. The Oregon Coast taught me that, because I knew the seafood was fresh there, and I still had the extreme reaction.

I spoke to one of my many doctors who told me to deal with it by avoiding seafood. Thanks, buddy. Yeah. I'll do that.

It turns out, though, that there are no reliable tests for food allergies. Discovering them is a process of elimination (in more ways than one), and if you feel better, then you're allergic to the food. (Or at least have a major sensitivity.)

Some of the other allergies that I had revealed themselves when I tried the food. I got very sick almost immediately.

One, though, was a real problem.

I was raised in Wisconsin. The dairy state. My parents (and the entire state for that matter) believed milk to be a miracle food. It was the healthiest thing in the world. Yet I was the baby who couldn't handle cow's milk, who needed formula. I was the kid who begged my friend's family to leave cheese off the pizza because I knew that cheese upset my stomach. I was the kid who never wanted ice cream with her chocolate cake.

I figured, as I got older, that I was lactose intolerant. So one afternoon when I was in my forties, I went to WebMD and looked up the symptoms for lactose intolerance…and realized I had a *severe* dairy allergy. Everything that they listed under severe allergy I had and then some.

Well, that explained doctors who thought I had differing varieties of stomach ailments, which never did show up on tests. From inflammatory bowel disease to ulcers, docs thought I had everything—and never figured out why my stomach constantly ached and I often had other issues after eating certain foods.

At best, I got headaches and migraines from the foods I was allergic to. At worse, well, really, I should have gone to the hospital more than I did.

Once I cut out dairy—and that's hard in America, since they put dairy in *everything* (from meat to plump it up [even raw meat like turkeys] to dried fruit to soups to…oh, never mind)—I got instantly healthier. I mean damn near overnight. My stomach stopped hurting. I dropped ten pounds of inflammation in a week. And I had more energy than I'd ever had.

I had no idea that it was *normal* for people to have *no* reaction after they ate. I had a sore stomach at best, and severe pains at worst. Those symptoms show back up immediately if I have anything that even touches a dairy product.

That was ten years ago, and it made me better. Except that occasionally, I would still get weirdly ill.

Turns out that some medications have dairy in their coating. Others have coating made of shellfish. And some drug manufacturers were later sued for failing to disclose that they had used shellfish or some other allergen in their product. They were sued because people died due to their negligence. I simply got sick.

Although about five years ago, I nearly died as well from continual poison from one of the supplements I was taking. Fortunately I had learned about eliminating parts of my diet to discover the problem, and the moment I eliminated that supplement, I got better.

I now look at the ingredients for *everything*. Anything I ingest gets examined and if I don't know what something is or if it has vague descriptions ("spices" "natural flavors") I don't eat it. That simple. And that hard.

Figuring out the food allergies made me healthier as my environment made me sicker.

I lived on the Oregon Coast, which is damp all of the time. Every building smells of mold or mildew. The house we bought had a leaky roof, and over time, we believe we ended up with a serious mold problem. Not black mold—we were on the lookout for that—but regular ordinary mold (if there is such a thing). And, it turns out, that not everyone gets affected the same way by regular ordinary mold. Someone in the household could get sick while someone else would be just fine.

Me, the person with all the allergies, I got sicker and sicker. Plus, the restaurants we went to couldn't accommodate my food allergies. ("Oh, we're sorry. We had no idea that butter was dairy.") I couldn't eat out any more. And the grocery stores in that 7,000-person town didn't carry non-processed foods. I had to order from Amazon or buy at a store over two hours away.

It was untenable. And I got worse and worse and worse, until after one of our workshops, I completely collapsed. The students are always great, acquiescing to our request that they not wear fragrances or use scented laundry soap. But the hotel where we held the workshop authorized construction right next to us, and used so many airborne chemicals that others (not just me) got really ill.

I didn't recover. And it became clear that I had to leave that town. I needed (I thought) major medical assistance. I no longer even had a GP, because the guy who had been my GP was fired for overprescribing opioids. The hospital misdiagnosed a friend's heart attack, and Dean's pneumonia, and a lot of other truly obvious things.

I needed something more than that. I needed a major city. But Dean and I have different ideas of city comfort. I hate the small cities of the west—Portland, Boise—and he hates humidity in the summer, which ruled out most of the country. He wouldn't live in California, and I didn't like Denver. We couldn't afford New York City.

Both of us wanted to live in a walkable area, not suburbs, which meant a downtown. And the only place with a thriving —or at least growing—downtown that we agreed on was Las Vegas.

Dean was visiting with friends in January of 2018, before the disastrous workshop. We were talking about finding properties to move to, knowing it was coming. He found us a lovely condo in a downtown building, and began the process of purchasing it. Our closing was the end of April, and then we'd start the arduous process of moving. At that point, we thought we would live half-time in Oregon and half-time in Las Vegas. (Winters in Las Vegas; summers on the cool Oregon Coast.) We'd sell our big house and move slowly, maybe buy something else on the Oregon Coast.

Then that disastrous workshop, and my health had gotten to the point of crisis (I'm not going to detail it, only to say... well, it was awful). We contacted our building in Las Vegas, and moved up our plans.

We arrived at a condo I hadn't seen in a part of the city I hadn't been in for fifteen years in early March. I barely made it through the drive. One hotel we had to stay at along the way used Febreze in their guaranteed allergy clean rooms. Febreze, for those of you who don't know, is scented chemicals and I'm so allergic to that I get sick after one sniff.

We managed to find another hotel in the same town at two a.m., but not after contemplating sleeping in our van that night. Those little travel surprises happen to me (and those of us with fragrance/chemical allergies) all the time. Which is why I can't travel.

The condo complex cleaned our new place with no chemicals. Steam on the carpets, vinegar in the water, and the place gleamed. The walls are concrete, and we have our own HVAC so we don't breathe anyone else's air.

We bought new furniture so we didn't bring any of the mold with us. Dean left me behind, then drove the cats down. He was gone for about five days—which took real courage, considering how sick I had been. He wasn't sure I'd make it through those days.

But I didn't just improve when we moved here. I improved *rapidly*. That process of elimination thing—guess what? I was allergic to the entire moldy environment of the Oregon Coast. Plus, I was finally getting good nutrition. The grocery stores here carry what I need, and most restaurants have vegan (non-dairy) options.

I have a normal life, suddenly. The hormones have eased now that I'm almost sixty. The migraines are never severe and come about once per quarter, if I have them at all.

But...and this is a big but...I can get really ill at the drop of a hat. Two weeks ago (as I write this), I opened the door to the condo to grab our newspaper, and got nailed by some Febreze. Someone—and I have no idea who—sprayed that crap in the hallway, and the smell gathered outside our place.

I was sick all day—migraine, the whole shebang. Although it was a mild migraine, because it wasn't compounding on the other allergies. And the other problems (except for the closed air passages) were less severe as well.

If I do the proper self-care, I'm mostly fine. Except when something icky ambushes me.

But I'll be honest: I'm unwilling to go somewhere else. I don't want to stay overnight anywhere except home because of all the chemicals, the pillow-sniffing, the booby-traps in the environment. And I have no guarantee that I can eat in those places. Las Vegas is one of the most vegan-friendly cities in the nation.

The air here is dry, and the buildings all have spectacular airflow. So if some idiot wearing an entire bottle of Axe Body Spray enters a restaurant that I'm in, I don't have to flee for my life. I just have to make sure I'm not sitting right next to the stinky fellow.

This miraculous sudden health has given me a heck of a perspective on how sick I had been, the compromises I made to get things done, and just how focused I had been to get as much done as I had.

Those things are the things I'll be sharing in the second half of this book.

I don't think of myself as "healed." I'm not. I still have chronic health problems. But I manage them. I have no idea if I have other health issues caused by all those years of exposure. This next year is all about discovering where my health is strong and if parts of it got compromised, as well as what I need to do to remain healthy.

And part of this next year is also about figuring out how to *be* healthier. It's a whole different lifestyle, and one I'm constantly surprised at.

So there. You got the short version of my health history (with a ton of stuff left out).

It's still soggy and rainy. I finished writing this in one of my favorite restaurants, which is colder than usual. (They normally bake so much they keep the heat off. Today, they can't keep up.) Locals are exclaiming about how wet they are, and some aren't sure how to close an umbrella.

It's amusing and different, but I'll be glad when the sun returns—and with it, a real clear sense that I'm in a different place, one that's better for me than almost any place I've lived before. And also, with that sense, an acknowledgement of how lucky I am that we stumbled on the right place for us both to live. Us—and the cats—who are also thriving.

We're all doing better, and I'm deeply grateful for that.

BEST-LAID PLANS OF MICE AND KITTENS
FINISHED MARCH 10, 2018

Written about four days before we got in the car to move to Las Vegas. Here's the update on the projects mentioned below: I finished the branding book, now called Creating Your Author Brand, *in the first week we were in Nevada. I finally finished the big Diving project, now called* The Renegat, *in August. The rest...well, you'll see in other posts.*

I started into this year going gangbusters. I had a big Diving project, which I figured I would finish in early March, some research to do on my next big project, and I would finish something smaller in between.

Those of you who support me on Patreon saw a flurry of blogs in the front of the year, and then I've been trickling the blogs out slowly ever since. That's not how I planned the year.

Plus, I have a few other projects to finish—the branding book is one—and a lot of updating to do on websites and such. I had started all of that, going fast, when…

Well, that chronic health condition of mine didn't just flare up. It overtook my life.

Dean and I realized that we needed to get me to a major city, where I'm closer to doctors who can deal with my everyday. (I am currently three and a half hours away from the experts who know what they're doing with the various health concerns.) I had several rather frightening flare-ups, one during the anthology workshop, and some of them are environmental.

We had known that I needed to get out of Lincoln City as my permanent residence, but we figured that would happen someday.

Turned out, someday is now.

Dean and I have bought a place in Las Vegas, where we will be part time. (We're planning for summers here, where it's cool.) The businesses will remain here, including WMG. The stores are doing very well. Everything is going well…except me.

No need to worry about my health. We're taking care of it all, and getting me out of the environment that makes the condition worse. So, we're doing the right things.

I'm very fortunate that there are right things to do. Many of you have written to me about your own chronic health conditions. Some of those conditions make mine seem like child's play. I always marvel at how determined you all are to write, publish, and share yourselves despite the barriers that you have to overcome. You inspire me.

My current writing barrier isn't my health—except peripherally. I've learned to write when the condition flares up. I know how much I can do, when the best times of day are, and what I can do to make the condition less intrusive in my life. It has taken years to get here, but I figured it out.

Nope, my writing barrier is the move itself.

We had to move up the move (no pun intended) from early May to mid-March because of some environmental factors. My neighbor is having a fight with the city and the local dump, so instead of paying to have his garbage carted away, he's burning it. In his fireplace. And I'm getting sicker by the day.

We had been talking about selling our big house and downsizing here in Lincoln City as well, and that feud cemented that decision. So we're selling the big house, and moving into about three separate places (Vegas, a smaller place in Lincoln City, and moving the stuff we don't want to our various stores.)

Since we were already planning to leave, we just moved up the timetable to get me out of here sooner. Dean will return after dropping me in Vegas, to organize and finish the bigger parts of the move. (With luck, by then the neighbor problem will be resolved.)

All of this sounds so easy. It's not. I'm Distract-O-Girl. I would have had this blog finished an hour ago, except that I paused to sort some books, then packed a box with cat items for the second trip (not this trip), notified a few people who needed to deal with some things here, and put items on the calendar for Dean for Monday.

I'm not doing anything that requires a lot of concentration right now, which is why this post will be short and won't involve analysis. There's no analysis that I can sustain for more than five minutes. (I'm Googling the weather for the trip, for heaven's sake. And looking at cat pictures. Because...you know...cat pictures.)

Normally, I push myself to write even when life gets in the way. But there are some events that simply take over everything.

I talk to a lot of you who deal with this, particularly when you're grieving for a loved one. (That process hijacks your brain; there's little you can do until the brain returns from its reset.) I've learned over the years when it's time to throw in the towel and promise myself that I will get back to fiction later.

Right now, I can't sustain it—and I don't want to. I need to focus on—oh, crap! I'm the only one who knows where those cat supplies are. I'd better put them here. And oh, yeah! I promised I'd give this particular thing to that particular person. Better do it right now, before I forget.

I'm sending emails with the header: *Before I forget* almost hourly. Because we moved this up, so the nice orderly way of doing things that we had planned for isn't going to be orderly at all. And it doesn't help that I get brain fog whenever my neighbor gets home from work and throws junk in his fireplace.

I have some projects I can work on once we're on the road. I also have projects I can work on while I'm unpacking and getting settled. Once I get settled, I'll be back to writing fiction. I should be at full speed when I have to teach an in-person workshop in late April. Which will feel good. I always write while the students are writing, so I'll be on course.

I'd call this a process blog, but it's really too scattered to be a "process." More like an update blog—and a reminder to all of you going through major life events that sometimes the best thing to do is focus on the life event, rather than try to force yourself to do everything.

And writing that made me remember that I need to back up some negotiation stuff that I had been putting off. Not to mention moving some files to a different room, so they don't get inadvertently included in a pile of boxes heading south, and…

You get the idea.

SETTLING IN: (A PROCESS BLOG)
FINISHED MARCH 26, 2018

I had forgotten how disruptive moving is. I am currently sitting on the new Elizabeth George hardcover that got delivered to our Vegas home last week, and typing on the Bluetooth keyboard on the kitchen table. The laptop sits on top of two Jill Shalvis books to get it at the right height as well, although I am looking down, so I probably need another book in there. But that makes the laptop unstable.

I don't want to stand. (I brought my laptop standing desk.) I've been standing a lot, because for the first week, chairs were at a premium in this place—as in, we didn't have any. We had brought the bed, but not chairs (we only had so much room in our van).

When you do a quick emergency move, you take what you can. It's been fun, but now it's time to settle in and get some work done.

I do love it here. My health has cleared up dramatically. That was unexpected. We figured it would take a lot more time to clear up. All that remains are some seasonal allergies that are, surprisingly, the same here in the desert as they are on the Oregon Coast.

The change of venue was good. I'm eating better (much better) and have a lot more energy. I also feel like a fog has lifted from my brain.

But I'm in transition. My writing office is a mess. Broken down boxes of new stuff that will become (or has become) shelves and balcony furniture and other condo-specific stuff.

The new desk remains in a box at the moment. My desk chair is in Lincoln City. (The old desk is too big for the space.) The cats also remain in Lincoln City, but Dean is bringing them down (by himself, courageous man) mid-week. In fact, by the time you read this, the room should look different. It should have cats, husband, and a chair…maybe.

Suffice to say, right now, I'm making do.

When we decided to make this transition, I had planned to use the laptop most of the time. I will be writing in various venues citywide. The condo is small, the city is big, and I've been trapped in a tiny town for years and years. I want to see people.

I've already done some work in various venues around town, and that works beautifully. In fact, in my copious spare time, I finished my draft of the branding book. It doesn't have a title yet, but it will. (I punted that to Allyson and the team at WMG. I want a sales-worthy title, and *The Branding Book* ain't it.)

I could work on that book while I was in the middle of organizing this place, because assembling a book from blogs was much easier than trying to use part of my brain to write something from scratch. I started the assembly over the Siskiyou Mountain Range, and stopped my work only when the rain turned into an unexpected snowstorm. Dean needed help driving (navigation, watching for idiots who thought snow was like dry pavement, that sort of thing). I continued work throughout California, and then did more once we got here, usually when I went to get us lunch or steal an hour here and there.

Even though this is only the second time I've done a cross-country move (as an adult), it's not my first move. I know that my brain goes to tilt. That's why I wrote two blog posts just before we left, and then got all the materials for the branding book into place so I could work on the three-day drive.

I had planned to finish the branding book before we got to Vegas. That didn't work, for a variety of reasons (not the least of which was an adventure in the middle of the night with a hotel that didn't provide the promised allergy-free room [and that reminds me. I need to put up a Yelp review because that night was extreme]). I continued once I got here, but things would get in the way.

No chairs, for one. Setup taking forever. I am not getting to this blog until Sunday, March 25, because I had to organize, prioritize, and then set up a few things. It took over an hour to set up the printer. I'm still missing a USB cable, so I can only operate the printer with my phone (!), so that's a bit irritating but not as bad as heading to the nearest Fed Ex Office to print things out.

I finally had to do something I didn't want to do: I had to commandeer the table in our main living area as my desk. I needed to put my calendars in order. And, ironically for a woman who has five calendars (in paper) and one on her computer, I forgot to back up the online calendar onto the new laptop. (I left the old writing computer, which is not networked, in Lincoln City.) So I had to spend much of Friday reassembling my calendar…after I finished the branding book.

Getting organized is becoming very important. I have three movie/TV deals in various stages, and every single one of them had a *deal with me now* moment during the move. (Silence for a month [three months in the case of one] and then, *Do It Now!* while I was on the road.) I need to figure out where the paperwork goes, because I don't have a filing system in place, and the all-important paper files for those deals are still in Lincoln City. (I figured they could come in the second wave, with the cats.) I have the computer files, but that's not quite the same. I like to eyeball contract terms on paper, as well as online, to make sure I haven't missed anything.

Which reminds me…I have to sign and scan a document. Excuse me while I figure out how the damn scanner works.

Thirty minutes later…

Okay, not all of that was the scanner. In fact, scanning took ten minutes. Plus time to print the paper file. Then five minutes to brag to Dean that I got it all to work. Then time to email the person in question, and (Distract-O-Girl) to answer other important email, and resist the impulse to check my website, and social media accounts.

That's how this has gone for the past week. One action leads to an unexpected and unpredicted action (Oh, yeah! Do this now before I forget!), which leads to another action, and then the project at hand becomes the forgotten project.

As I said, this isn't my first major move, so I expected this. I did meet my extreme deadline (the branding book, which will be in a bundle in May), but I have no other extreme deadlines, so I have the luxury of working in my alter ego Distract-O-Girl. I have deadlines on editing and on teaching, which I will get to later tonight.

But this post is the next deadline. And I hope to get back to the Diving novel (!) tomorrow.

So, how do I make this process blog useful to you all?

Well, let's start with expectations.

I knew the moment the move became a reality that I would

lose at least a few days if not weeks to the move itself. Initially, the move was planned for the end of April. With a planned move, it's easier to plan work. It's also easier to pack.

But because of our idiot neighbor, we got me out of Lincoln City sooner. (And because I mentioned it on Facebook, two locals with a bit of power are now aware of the issue. They have more clout than idiot neighbor in our small town, so maybe something will [finally] be done, and Dean won't have to breathe the fumes while he packs.) Changing the date by forty-five days meant much was undone, and I didn't get to finish projects ahead of time.

I had to set aside the established deadlines and be realistic with myself. There was no way to get much of this work finished in any kind of timely manner.

Kris pauses to contemplate the balcony. Realizes the pollen count is too high to sit out there comfortably. Pouts. Continues.

So, before we left, I made a paper list and a list on my computer of everything that had to be done ASAP. That included making sublists, for Dean, so he would know what to pack with the cats (that couldn't be packed ahead of time), and making sure everyone who needed to know about the changes did know.

On that list were all the writing and editing projects that absolutely had to be done by the end of March. Only one writing project really, objectively, needed to be done. The branding book. I also needed three blogs (from the moment I started that list.) I wrote two of them in Lincoln City.

This is the third.

I have several reading projects that I had to do, plus I have some line editing that needs to be done. The paper manuscript for the line edit is in a box around here somewhere. I don't have to get to that until April if I want to push the deadline.

If you look at my paper calendar from January/February,

you'll see all kinds of other important deadlines, including promoting the current Storybundle that I'm in (a cool one about Femmes Fatales), deadlines I decided I could set aside until I got settled in.

I am slowly hauling those deadlines back out, and seeing if meeting them is realistic.

By taking the deadline pressure off me, I was and am able to concentrate more fully on the move. I can allow those distractions to happen, and I get a lot less frustrated by things like that missing USB cable for the printer. I'm also a lot more accepting of things getting in the way of the writing. If I need to make an unplanned shopping run for cleaning supplies, it doesn't feel like an imposition. It feels like something I'm doing to get settled.

The move will have this kind of impact on me and my writing for the next six to nine months, as I learn the rhythm of this life change. How does the weather in Vegas change my habits? (I expect it will quite a bit come summer.) How does all the work remaining in Lincoln City get done on short trips north? Or do I live by laptop now? (I vote laptop.)

So…I managed my own expectations.

I'm also managing the expectations of others. I have an out-of-the-office message on my email that allows me to ignore less pressing emails until I have the time. The message also explains to the people I'm doing major business with why I'm not answering them as fast as usual, so it makes them more patient—and takes some pressure off me.

Maybe you're seeing a theme here. I'm taking pressure off me as much as possible.

I'm doing that because moving is a major cause of stress. Back when I moved across country the first time, the so-called experts said that moving was in the top ten causes of stress.

Now, the so-called experts list other things first. But they still put moving high on that stressors list.

One major reason for the stress? The loss of routine. I knew I was going to be stressed from the start of this move. I'm less stressed than I would have been, because I planned.

(But, looking at articles about stress and the loss of routine, I realized my poor cats are going to be damn near traumatized for the next month. Ten days of no me, no Dean, then Dean gets home, no me [no routines], then they get bundled into a car and driven for seventeen-plus hours to a strange place with only a bit of their stuff, and no familiar routines...Oh, joy. That'll be fun for all of us.)

I'm not setting up proper routines yet, because I don't have a car. I also need a better time of day to run. It's not going to be a problem in the summer, since I'll be heading to an indoor track, but for the next few weeks, anyway, before the weather gets too hot for Coastie me, I'll need to figure out what, exactly, the routine is.

I also need to set up a good writing routine, but I can't do that fully until I have an office. Even though I'll be using my laptop, I need a home base for calendars, papers, projects, and general mess (I'm one of those people).

I'm not sure if my word count will increase or decrease, but I'm not worried about it at all. I'm concentrated on *projects* at the moment. All of them, those concerning moving and unpacking, and those concerning the writing/editing/reading.

The key for me (and anyone in this situation) is to avoid piling more stress on top of the existing stress. Also, to take a moment to appreciate the changes that have occurred.

I'm lucky enough that I could just pick up my life and move when we realized that my idiot neighbor was poisoning me. I know how very lucky I am, and I know that most people couldn't leave home/job/community on such short notice.

Because I have a non-traditional career—and have had one all of my life—I've done this pick-up and go thing twice. (The first time was in my twenties.)

It's not ideal, but it's certainly not something to complain about. It's actually something to celebrate. I know how fortunate I am.

I have a lot to learn, a lot of organizing to do, and a lot of things to catch up on, not the least of which are the changes in publishing in 2018. I looked at some of those articles today for the first time in a month.

So, I'm settling in. And it feels good, albeit odd, since I had no idea on January 1st that I would be in our own place in Las Vegas in March.

As I said a couple of weeks ago, best laid plans…

Thanks for all the support and kind notes during this time.

SCHEDULES AND STRUCTURE
FINISHED APRIL 23, 2018

The in-person Oregon Coast writing workshop ended on Saturday, and worked relatively well, considering all the things we had to do to deal with my unexpected need to remain here in Vegas. Some things worked as usual, and others didn't. Surprisingly for me, I ended up as tired on Sunday as I usually am when I am talking with everyone in person. I think that means the video-conferencing worked, and I felt like I was in the room. (I ended up towering over everyone—one of those larger-than-life screens, so for the students I was definitely a presence...)

I made myself take Sunday off completely. I wandered to a favorite restaurant, discovered a part of Vegas that reminds me of Eugene, Oregon, and read a book that wasn't an assignment for anything. Promising myself every single time I got nervous about all the things I had to do that I would deal with them on Monday.

It's no wonder I woke up panicked Monday morning.

But in the middle of that panic, I realized something, which made me shake my head and giggle at myself. I'd been deliberately avoiding setting a schedule until *after* the workshop.

There were a lot of personal reasons for that which I won't delve into. A few involved the original timing of the move—we planned to leave after the workshop, instead of more than a month before. But mostly, I realized when I arrived in Vegas that I wouldn't have the opportunity for a regular schedule until the workshop ended.

By then, I wouldn't be reading assigned books and working on planning. I would have an office, which I do more or less. (More less than more; right now I'm writing on the desk, using a standing laptop desk for my cup of ice tea, a box as a bookshelf, and a really wobbly table for the printer—which Gavin the cat absolutely loves.)

The transition continues, but I have to hunker down and return to full-time work. A number of you have told me to take it easy for anywhere from six months to a year, but I hate to tell you, that says more about you than me.

Imagine if I moved to Vegas because I had a new day job. If I was a lucky person, I'd be able to take two weeks between the old job and the new job to make the move and the transition. Unlucky folks get an entire weekend to travel across country.

In other words, I would have already been putting in my forty hours per week, starting about a month ago.

When I ramped up for the workshop—which requires me to work about fifteen hours per day—I went back to my old workshop schedule. I wrote in the morning, kept exercising, and did all of the workshop work as well. Two differences made it tougher here—I had to exercise in the morning as well, due to the heat that I'm not yet acclimatized to, and the fact that Dean, who usually acts as my backup on food and other errands, wasn't here. So I worked harder here, and it felt good.

It was the workshop schedule that made me have my realization this morning. The panic wasn't coming from all of the work I had assigned myself after the workshop; it was coming from the loss of the schedule.

For decades, Dean and I have warned newly minted full-time freelancers that they will get less done when they quit their day jobs. Dean also warned an attorney friend of his, who reduced his private legal practice so he could work at home.

It's not that home has more distractions. In some ways, it has fewer distractions—no colleagues to talk to when you're restless, no gossip to share, no one to go to lunch with—but it also has no set structure.

I've been giving that advice so often that I've blogged about it as well. I think the first time was nine years ago, in a blog that eventually became part of my *Freelancer's Survival Guide*.

I wrote:

You had a schedule at your day job, but someone else imposed it on you. Now you need to design your own—and post it on the door to your (home) office.

Stick to this schedule, but make it realistic.

I haven't had a day job in 100,000 years. But I have had a schedule, a religious one that I stuck to year in and year out. Much of it was built around Lincoln City specific events, like our Sunday writer's lunch and our weekly meetings at WMG. Some of it was Lincoln City weather, which is darker and grayer and colder than it is here in Vegas. So running outside late in the day when the traffic was thin and the light was better (from the west) made a lot of sense in Lincoln City. But a lot of my schedule was built around Dean as well. We have dinner together, and we always consult about our day.

He's only here part time right now, and wasn't here hardly at all in April. I was on my own there. There is no Sunday writer's lunch and the meetings at WMG are catch-as-catch-can by phone. Las Vegas weather is warmer and sunnier, and if

I'm going to continue running outside for another month or so (before the heat of the summer), I have to do so early in the day (or rather, early for me).

In other words, that long-honed schedule went away—the same as a schedule long-honed by a day job vanishes the moment you quit the job.

Who knew?

I'd been muttering that I needed to set my schedule. I'd organize a workday, but somehow held two contradictory thoughts in my head at the same time. I seemed to believe I could continue with my old schedule while adapting to my new environment.

It wasn't until Monday morning, when I looked to the future and realized I had only three scheduled things on my calendar, that I suddenly understood what I was suffering from.

I have a lack of structure. Me! The woman whose superpower is structure.

No wonder I felt at loose ends both before and after the workshop.

You can't build a new structure in a day. Nor can I build my final structure until Dean gets here full time, which will be by August (if our plans work as we hope).

But I can set up a few more regularly scheduled events now that the workshop is behind me. There are some classes I'm looking at, both at the gym I've joined and at some organizations around town. Those will give me structure, as will all the upcoming visits by friends.

On Friday, toward the end of the workshop, my brain also offered up a solution to a problem I'd been noodling with. I didn't want to be stuck writing at home all the time. Shortly after we moved, my gigantic desktop computer died a terrible death. I could have replaced it with another gigantic desktop, but I balked—although not at the price. At the stationary equipment. I already had a new laptop, and I wanted nothing more than another new laptop.

One to stay home and the other to travel with me wherever I go.

I just hadn't figured out where I would go.

Friday, my brain solved that for me. I'm not going to list the exact solution, because I don't want to be findable, but it mostly has to do with working in various parts of the city, in a bunch of venues that don't care if you hog a table or a desk or a bench for an hour or two or three. Some of those venues are walking distance, and some will require a drive, which doesn't bother me at all.

I'd been slowly groping my way toward a structure without realizing that was what I was doing.

Now that I know what the problem is, I know how to fix it. What made me giggle was that I had missed the problem altogether. I'd written out lists because lists usually work for me. But they didn't here. I met every deadline I had and then some. I gave myself a pass because I had just moved, and I had health issues. But I knew I was missing something.

What I was missing was what I had warned countless writers and all of you about for years. When your overall life structure changes, your productivity goes down until you build a new structure.

Well, duh. And yet, I had missed that.

All because of one simple phrase: "day job." I didn't have one, so I couldn't have the standard *quitting your day job* problems, right?

I'm still giggling. Those peals of laughter you're hearing are from me, realizing just how much we writers can lie to ourselves. How much I still lie to myself.

I thought the problem was complicated. It's a simple

problem with a complicated solution, one that will take patience as I set up the new life down here.

I have never had much patience, but I do have determination. And I've set up structures many, many, many times before. This is something I can do.

And lo and behold, once I made that realization, the panic left and the amusement arrived.

Off I go to figure out the next few months. Excuse me now, while I commune with my calendars.

THRIVING DESPITE...
FINISHED AUGUST 24, 2018

I planned to write this guest blog last night, but I got sick at the gym yesterday. Not call-in-an-ambulance sick. An oh-you-must-be-kidding-me sick. I suffer from severe allergies, which is one of the many reasons my husband and I moved to Las Vegas last March. Airflow is better here. The dry air is better for me. The food is better. And there are better doctors than the small town I lived in before.

But I still get nailed from time to time by careless people (whom I do not call "careless people" when I'm talking to anyone who knows my penchant for colorful language). Yesterday, it was a man who was wearing too much baby powder—so much you could smell him throughout half the gym. He actually left a baby powder stain after he sat on one of the carpeted benches on the running track.

I'm allergic to most fragrances and a whole bunch of other airborne chemicals. Apparently, baby powder in large amounts is one of those fragrances I'm allergic to. I went from running on the track to standing in a clear area trying to breathe.

The airflow fixed the problem soon enough, but the incident left me tired and debilitated for the rest of the evening. *Ironic*, I thought as I stood there, my throat half-closed from the guy's white powdery stench, *I haven't had an incident for more than a month, and then on the day I'm going to write this post...*

The incident was a reminder that while I've been feeling light-years better these last six months, I'll never be cured.

I have had these allergies and chronic migraines and other not-easy-to-solve health problems most of my adult life. Things got so bad in the past two years that I could do very few things, and usually early in the day.

So I worked out systems. I was better in the early afternoon since it takes me forever to wake up in the morning. I would write, then I would run, and then I would read. I set quotas. I had a word count to hit every day, a distance to hit on my run, and a set number of pages to read every night.

But those quotas had asterisks. If I had a migraine, I would write until my brain turned to mush. If I had some kind of allergy issue, I would strive for an hour. If I couldn't run, I could still hit my 10,000 steps—even if I just stumbled from wall to wall in my living room, occasionally sitting down to prevent myself from fainting with dizziness. If I couldn't read, I would watch (or listen to) stories on television.

Sounds harsh, I know. But I had learned a few things in my life. First, exercise. It makes all of my conditions better. Since I started exercising about ten years ago, the number of sick days went down. So those 10,000 steps have been part of my daily life—with only two misses—since 2012. Writing keeps me sane, so I do as much as I can—nonfiction if I can't write fiction. Reading is as necessary as breathing for me, but I realized in my twenties that storytelling can substitute for reading if need be. So me and my pillow on the couch, having movie marathons, became a common thing, particularly in my 30s. I had migraines twenty-one out of twenty-eight days every month—while I was writing six books per year and editing *The Magazine of Fantasy & Science Fiction*.

Fortunately, I worked at home. I didn't have to go to an office (since there were days I couldn't drive) and I could pick the hours I was clearheaded to get something done, rather than adhere to a nine to five. In my twenties, I worked as the news director of a radio station, and I split my shift five a.m. to ten a.m., then four p.m. to seven p.m. If I had migraines then (and I did, a lot), I would "indulge" them in the afternoon when I was off. It became pretty clear to me pretty fast that I couldn't maintain that forever.

But the writing, reading, exercise thing? I did that for decades, literally, as doctors helped me figure out what triggered migraines (and what mitigated them) and as I slowly learned what my allergies were. I am much healthier now than I've ever been, which is creating its own problems.

You see, now I don't know how to rest. I was always forced to rest, so I would save all my rest activities for the days when I couldn't do anything else. Now, I rarely have to rest because of illness. Now, I have to rest when I exhaust myself because I feel so dang good.

But days like yesterday remind me that I will always have these issues. I know how to cope with bad days. I used to have more of them than good days.

Self-care is what got me to more good days than bad. I have to be diligent about what I eat, and how long I sleep. I need to exercise every single day. I need to flee a room immediately when someone with too much cologne enters. I have long since stopped apologizing for my weird behavior. If I have to leave, I do. If I can't eat in a particular restaurant, I say so. If I have a migraine, I'm clear about whether or not I can work or drive or socialize.

Some of that comes from being older, and living with this

stuff for decades. But much of it comes from the (slow for me) realization that getting mad at the condition doesn't help. Finding work-arounds does. And sometimes, that quiet day on the couch watching six movies is necessary—even for the healthy version of me.

Rest and doing something else is important.

Because if I do that, and eat right and exercise daily, I can write more. Read more. Enjoy my life more.

And that's what really counts.

THE GENERAL USEFUL STUFF

THE STRUCTURE OF THIS SECTION

This section provides the meat of the book. Some of you have read the previous section and know my personal journey. The rest of you only want the how-to. I get it. That's usually what I want too.

My nonfiction writing style is colloquial. I am writing this section from my own personal experience as someone who suffers from chronic illness. I am not an expert, except in my own body and my own methods. I am sharing them, and my attitude toward what I do with you, not to tell you what to do, but to show how I do it.

Normally, when I write my business blog, I cite experts and current articles. I'm not going to do so in this book. I don't feel comfortable evaluating experts here, because this isn't about the business of writing or about writing craft, which I am an expert in. This is about health, and while I like to think I'm smart about health stuff, I'm probably as susceptible to crackpot ideas as the next person. I'd rather just rely on my own experience, and let you accept or reject it on your own.

Here's the caveat, though: I am not a health professional. I am writing from my own experience only, and providing my personal information here as an example, not as a recommendation that you do everything I do.

I write forcefully because I speak forcefully. In here, you will see my recommendations and advice, and it will be written in command language: do this; do that. I am not going to add the lighter words "if you think it's right for you," to every sentence, but those words are implied in each piece.

Whatever you take from this book, make sure that those things are the best things for you. You and I are different people, so we have different reactions to things. Experiment, try my method, or reject it out of hand. That's up to you. I respect whatever decision you make.

Finally, the structure in this section. I have written many of the chapters here for this book. A couple of the chapters come from older blog posts, because I feel like they made my point.

All of the chapters have the date I finished them underneath the title. So, if you're a regular reader of my nonfiction, you will know what you have encountered before and what's new.

I do change my mind about what works and what doesn't, especially in the business of writing. You'll find some of that older stuff on my website, but you won't find any of it here. If an older piece is part of this book, that piece is here because I still believe what I wrote.

I hope you find some of my methods useful. Here they are.

PRIORITIES
FINISHED ON FEBRUARY 16, 2019

I write a lot. I always have. When I was in college, I wrote essays instead of taking tests, wrote fiction, and worked as a freelance nonfiction writer. I also worked in the news department of a listener-sponsored radio station, where we reported and wrote a half-hour newscast. I did that twice a week on top of everything else.

Nowadays, I write books, nonfiction, and short stories. I don't have a target weekly word count, but I do put in time, almost daily. I'm generally disappointed if I get only 1,000 words in a day, and super pleased if I get over 5,000.

Remember, I only count *new* words, not rewrites or anything else. All of that happens at other times, not during my writing time.

My writing has been the constant in my life. I took writing classes in college, not to learn from the instructors (most of whom had less success than I did even then) but because I needed to block out time for writing in my busy life, and I knew myself well enough to understand that if I was writing for a class, I would block out time every week.

Mind games. Writing is all about mind games and understanding yourself.

Even though I don't understand myself as well as I think I do.

For years, I would say that I get so much writing done because I have no life. Turns out that was true. Due to the constrained circumstances I lived in on the Oregon Coast, I had no life—or very little of one. I couldn't go out to movies or dinner with friends; I had no opportunity to see concerts or plays; I couldn't take in-person continuing education classes; and I couldn't make the one to two hour one-way drive that would take me to the bigger cities, because I couldn't guarantee I would make the ride home.

I had the time to write—when I was healthy, which was rare. So I learned how to write while ill.

The key, for me, turned out to be a structure I didn't have to think about. I knew what I needed to do—not in the deadline sense, but in the daily sense. It took me a long time to form that structure, but once I had it, I could function inside it almost instinctively. When my circumstances changed due to our move to Las Vegas in 2018, it took me weeks to realize that I had demolished my structure when I changed locations. I had to rebuild from scratch. (I deal with that in the chapter marked "Schedules" in the personal journey section.)

Rebuilding forced me to reexamine my priorities. I can't build a structure until I know what I put first, second, and third in my life. So, priorities before scheduling—or I'll blow everything up and get nothing done.

My priorities are relatively simple, because I don't have children or a day job. More on that below.

My priorities are:
1. My husband
2. My health
3. My writing

These are big broad categories that I use to cover a variety of things. I could as easily write them this way:
1. My family
2. My health
3. My career

I don't waiver in this order, for reasons I'll list below. I list family first because the one thing that life teaches in brutal ways is that our time with our loved ones is limited. We need to tend to our family first, in all ways. Realize though that family is whatever it means to you. For me, family is my husband and some of my closest friends. If they're in crisis, I'm there. If they need something, I'm there.

My husband and I interact daily, and we make sure we spend quality time together. We also are both writers, so we understand the demands writing puts on a relationship.

However, when he got seriously ill and needed care in the fall of 2017, I dropped the writing altogether to help him. I wasn't healthy enough myself to juggle both of our health demands, the household chores, and the other demands of illness without giving up something. The something was the least important thing on my priorities list—the writing.

Dean did the same thing for me last year. My health got so bad that we had no choice but to move immediately. He had to handle the bulk of all of it, although he had been handling the bulk of it anyway. He likened my chronic illness to us being two frogs in a puddle of water. Little did we realize we were in a pan of water, and the water was coming slowly to a boil.

By the end of that rough couple of years, Dean was doing most of everything. Then we moved me here, and he had to handle the move on his own. His writing, which is also third in his priority list, went out the window for a good part of 2018.

We all have times in our lives when we have to give up something on our priorities list. It isn't always because of an emergency. I strongly advise anyone with babies and small children to focus on them as much as possible. Children are little for only the blink of an eye. You'll never get to see that first step a second time or receive those joyful hugs that only a toddler can give once the kid hits grade school. Once the kids go to school, you can bring the writing back or make it rise on the priority list. You'll have time then.

This goes for parents who have jobs outside of the home as well as the kids' stay-at-home caregiver. Enjoy your kids while you have them with you.

And speaking of primary caregivers, sometimes we have to take care of our spouses or our parents or some other close relative. If you find yourself in that situation, remember the priority list. Family (however you define it) first, your health second. (Or maybe even your health first, family second.) The writing comes in as a distant, distant, distant third. You will get a chance later, if you take care of yourself as well as your loved one, to get back to the writing.

So, family first. The family is what makes us human. Family should also be a refuge. If you have a toxic nuclear family—like I did—then you need to redefine family to include friends or other loved ones. Sometimes family first means *separating* yourself from those harmful biological family members and finding your true family. It's a journey.

Remember that.

I put health second, even though many advisers say that you should always put your health first. It's that old thing they tell you on airlines—put on your oxygen mask first, then assist the person next to you.

That's good advice...except that those of us with chronic illness can misuse it. If we put illness and its care first, it can take over our lives much worse than it already has. Everyone in our lives ends up taking care of the illness instead of taking care of their relationships.

See the difference?

So, in my life at least, health is second. But a close second.

Because if I don't take care of my health, I can't function.

Thanks to our move, I'm in a lucky position. My health is better than it has been since I was a teenager. It's still not perfect. I can have an allergy attack after entering the wrong building or eating the wrong food. Those attacks can put me out of commission for hours or days or, in the past, weeks. So caution is my watchword, but at the moment, I'm better.

Last year at this time, I was not. I could barely function. The environment around me—the moldy house, the poor nutrition due to the lack of proper food in the area, and our lovely asshole neighbor who decided to burn his garbage—almost took me out.

Still, I maintained my routines and honestly, I think they saved my life.

Health for me is all about routines. Eight hours of sleep. Good food three times per day. (The small meals every few hours don't work for me.) Exercise.

Where I fall down is in relaxation, but I didn't realize that until I got healthier. More on that in a future chapter.

I also take prescribed medications at the same time every

day, as part of the routine, so I don't forget them. The more consistent I am, the better off I am.

So, when I talk about health, I am talking about *self-care*, in all of its permutations.

Let's break these down just a little.

Sleep: After I got mono at sixteen, I wasn't able to stay up all night any longer. I was that teenage kid who fell asleep at late night parties. I'm still not very good at shorting myself on sleep. I get migraines after two days of six hours or less of sleep—even at my age. So eight hours for sleep is essential for me.

Even though I suffer from insomnia. I've learned how to mitigate that too. If I can't sleep, I will lie in bed and rest. If I'm too restless for that, I get up and go through my pre-bed ritual all over again—after I've checked the temperature in the condo. If it's too cold or too hot, I can't sleep either. I don't panic when I can't sleep (or I'd be panicked several times per week). I reboot my rituals as if I was a computer, and start all over again.

I also learned the power of naps. Naps got me through the worst of my health problems. A twenty-minute nap is restorative when I'm healthy. A two-hour nap sometimes gets me through a bad migraine. An hour nap as the migraine comes on often mitigates the headache's power.

I've learned all of that through trial and error. But I'm willing to try. And if I need a nap, I drop everything and take the nap. No toughing it through the exhaustion, because that will lead to a health collapse. Better to find the twenty minutes than tough my way through a day and crater the following day.

Food: Three meals, no matter what. Three meals of food that's good for me. That was hard on the Oregon Coast, but really possible here in Las Vegas. I can eat to excess again, so it's something I have to watch. I try to keep my food intake balanced. I eat fresh ingredients whenever possible, partly because processed foods can often exacerbate my food allergies. But the food has to taste good and be something I enjoy. There's no way I'll stick to a food regimen if I don't enjoy it.

So food is a big part of my day—and my health.

Exercise: Because I now live in a walking city, I can combine food and exercise easily. I walk to at least one meal per day. I eat out a lot, but at vegan restaurants or restaurants that cater to people with dairy allergies. I eat small portions and take food home for another meal.

The walk to and from the restaurant adds steps to my total for the day.

Yep, I'm one of those wearables advocates. I bought a Fitbit in 2014 and discovered that striving for the magic 10,000 steps per day works for me. I lost ten pounds in the first three months of wearing the thing. I can do 10,000 steps, it seems, with a migraine (even if I'm shuffling around in the dark), with the flu (I'm not describing how that is possible), and even with a bum leg. I've been consistent with 10,000 steps, missing only twice since I got the Fitbit—once accidentally (that never happened again!) and once because I injured my knee so badly I couldn't walk. I had to reset my goal, and I did.

I was irritated to learn that exercise made me feel better. All those studies that say eating right and exercising will improve your health and mood? Those damn things are right. I wish they weren't, to be honest. It would be easier to sit on my butt and eat lots of bad-for-me stuff. But when I do that, I feel much, much worse.

So eating right and exercising makes me feel better. The other bonus is that I sleep better. (Yeah, also irritating.) And the third bonus? I have more energy. Even as my health declined, my energy level remained consistent because of my commitment to exercise.

I do all the other health related things I can, too, but not all at once. I make appointments with myself to make appointments. I hate them as much as the next person, so I schedule when I'll call for the appointment (if I can) and then I keep the appointment. I try not to have more than one check-up per month.

I also learned to get all of my vaccines. Since I started getting the flu shot, I haven't had a serious bout of flu. I might get a two-day sniffle, but that's it.

Keeping the health as good as possible helps with my third priority:

Writing.

Sometimes, when I was really, really sick, I had a word-count quota. Or an hours-at-the-desk quota. I try not to work with quotas, though, because I love to write. What's the point of doing it otherwise? All of my efforts are aimed at keeping the writing fun.

Except…I would rather be reading.

So, I have learned the hard way that reading is a *reward* for a good day's writing. The same with any other kind of story I could consume. No TV shows until I've written; no movie until I've written; no games until I've written.

I'll talk more in the next chapter how I manage to be productive even when I'm not feeling well. But the biggest key to that is realizing that writing is my third priority.

Sometimes I'll stumble around my condo or my neighborhood, grumping aloud at myself: *You're not writing, are you? Shouldn't you be writing?* And if I'm not tending to my health or doing something for my relationship with Dean, that complaint is a valid one. And one I need to listen to.

Sure, I would rather read a book or sometimes, I'd rather

clean the cat boxes than write. Especially if some project is going slowly.

Email isn't writing. Research isn't writing. Rewriting isn't writing. Only new words is writing.

Remembering that has made me prolific, even with all the health problems.

That and the fact that writing is third in my priority list. I will make everything and everyone else wait while I'm getting words. Even if I have an "important" phone call. Or a negotiation that needs to be completed. Or something else that "needs" to be done right this minute.

I find it useful to think of writing the way that people think about their day jobs. If your best friend called and asked you to come right over to help him with something, you'd go, right? Unless you were at work. Then you'd ask a series of questions about how serious the situation was. If he was on his way to the hospital and needed someone to watch his kid right now, you'd go, whether you were at work or not. But if he just needs help moving his car across town, then you wouldn't.

Writers often volunteer to help in both circumstances.

That little day job trick, which I figured out in my twenties, has kept me focused on my third priority really, really well. It's up to me, the writer, though. Because no one else is going to be able to keep track of what I do. I'm home much of the time. I have "free" time. I'm the logical person to call.

Until I say no a lot of times. Then some people learn to respect the boundaries. Not everyone, but most people.

That's the other thing about priorities. These are *my* priorities. They might not be yours. They certainly aren't everyone's.

I don't expect other people to have the same priorities that I do. It's up to me to prioritize my family, my health, and my writing. It's not up to the world. The world is what it is. Other people will do what they do.

I have learned to say no more than yes, to draw boundaries around important parts of my life, and to know both my strengths and my limitations.

And that helps me with the priorities.

It also helps with productivity, which is up next.

PRODUCTIVITY
FINISHED ON FEBRUARY 17, 2019

For my entire writing life, people have called me prolific. By the standards set by the modern publishing industry in the past twenty years, I am. But most prolific writers were stymied by the traditional publishing system, which couldn't handle more than one or two books per year from an author—any author. The traditional publishing system put in a series of checks and balances like revision requests, and publication dates more than one year out. To make matters worse, traditional publishers buy at most three books under one contract, and wait until the numbers are in on all three of them before buying any more. That slows a writer down—at least from the point of view of readers.

Many writers, me included, dealt with this big roadblock by writing under a variety of names. Even though I've retired many of my pen names or consolidated them under my real name (Rusch), I still have a few very active pen names. Of the ones I admit to, Kris Nelscott and Kristine Grayson have established careers and fan bases of their own. I couldn't retire those pen names if I wanted to.

From the outside, it seems like I write a lot. From inside my day-to-day existence, it seems like I don't write nearly enough. I constantly feel behind or overwhelmed or trapped by whatever project I'm working on. Every new idea becomes an oh-shiny!, and I want to work on that, until I get started, and then a different project becomes an oh-shiny!, much to my dismay.

I suspect that, ten years from now, my word counts and my habits won't seem prolific at all. I can already see young (in writing experience, not years) indie writers catapulting ahead of me on daily word count. Some of these writers will burn out, because they aren't managing their work/life balance—which is, in reality, those priorities I mentioned in the previous chapter.

But some of them are finding ways to be more prolific. Many of those ways have existed forever, or so it seems. My friend Kevin J. Anderson, whom I've known since college, has dictated his novels for decades. He has someone transcribe them—or he did before Dragon software—and then he edits the project.

A lot of writers use dictation software, training it to respond to their voice, and then producing 3,000 words or more in an hour. Which sounds great when you're focused on new words, but with the voice-recognition software comes an inevitable editing draft, just to make sure the paragraphs and punctuation are in the right place, and that the software understood you correctly. I can't get Siri to understand me for the length of a text, and that's after years of using voice commands for texting, so I worry about the editing part.

Not that I would ever dictate. I try it every now and then, and have since Kevin tried to get me to do it back in the 1980s. But I worked in radio long enough that my critical voice accompanies the sound of my voice, as close as the fingers are to the palm of my hand. If I want to write critically rather than creatively, then dictation is the way to do so.

I think, too, I'm reluctant to sacrifice my vocal talents to my writing career, especially since I'm planning to do a lot more work in audio and video in the next several years.

But that's personal for me, and tells you little about my methods.

How do (and did) I get work done, even with a chronic illness that, at its worst, incapacitated me twenty-one out of twenty-eight days every month?

Some of my methods were, and are, draconian. I once told the World's Greatest Doctor about them and she looked at me as if I was crazy. *Hard on yourself much?* she asked. I laughed and replied, *If I don't push, I would get nothing done at all.*

She was a doctor, who went through medical school and interning and residency and all of that horrendous stuff they put doctors through. She understood pushing. She just didn't recommend it for someone with health issues.

I don't blame her. As my husband would often point out, if I pushed too hard, I would be sick more rather than less. So the balance, for me, was finding a push that was hard, but not so hard that it would incapacitate me for days on end.

So let's see if I can break this down in ways that might help someone else.

First, let's go back to the priorities of the previous chapter. Family first, health second, and writing third.

When I was younger, I put writing second. That led to many more days incapacitated than I needed to suffer through. I finally acquiesced to my body and made my health a priority.

What that meant, in practical terms, was that there were days when I had to choose between getting new words done or completing my exercise. As a young woman, I chose words; as a middle-aged woman, I chose exercise—and was often rewarded with time to do words as well.

As I got sicker and sicker, time became the focus of my life. Time equaled energy for me. I only had so much energy per day, it seemed, and so I had to ration my time to accommodate that energy. In the ten years before our move, I could not do something different in a day without losing that day.

What do I mean? I mean that if I went to lunch with a friend, that was all I could do for a day. If I agreed to speak on someone's podcast, I could do nothing else that day.

It wasn't that I was lazy or that a podcast was a particularly hard thing to do.

It was that I only had about three hours of energy every day, and I had to acknowledge that. A podcast, one hour only, would put me flat on my butt afterwards, because I had to think on my feet, be gregarious, and remain present. Lunch held other dangers, like fragrance or food triggers that might make me sick for days. So in addition to the basic enjoyment of a conversation with my friend, I also had to be ultra vigilant, sniffing the air whenever someone new came into the restaurant so that I wouldn't get poisoned by the slow, low-grade stink of someone's cologne.

I literally had to choose between lunch or a movie or an interview, and writing. Often I had to choose between those things and exercise as well.

Needless to say, I became more and more of a recluse. And I turned down a lot of online interviews. In-person interviews had been out of the question for years.

So…time and energy.

They correlate for anyone with a chronic illness. The other thing I learned about time and energy and my illness was that there were, generally speaking, times of the day when I was more alert or energetic than other times. By evening, I would get brain fog and couldn't guarantee that I would be able to work—any kind of work, from nonfiction writing (which I find easier than fiction) to reading (for editing) to interviews or consuming story. I had to mentally block evenings off of my scheduled work time. Any evening I got was a bonus.

Mornings weren't great either when I lived in Oregon. Some of that was health. Much of it, I learned when I moved to the sunny desert, was the light. I now wake up early and with energy. In the darkness of the north, I would wake up and struggle through the first two hours of my morning, trying to ease myself into wakefulness. I know this was based on light because when we have the rare cloudy or rainy morning in Las Vegas, I can feel the difference. It takes me longer to become alert in the darkness of a cloudy day than it does in full sunshine.

Sunlamps help, but not as much as I had hoped they would.

So, mornings were something I had to ease into, and evenings were out of the question. Afternoons was my best work and exercise time.

I always prefer to write first, but living in the north in the winter meant that I only had a few hours of daylight. The small town I lived in had a rather mediocre health club with a running track so small that calling it a "track" is unfair to the goat path that it was. I loathe treadmills, although I used them early on in my exercise routine, before the Fitbit and the 10,000 steps. (The Fitbit quickly taught me that whatever I was doing on the treadmill, it wasn't exercise.)

I either walked to a destination or, in the later few years, I ran. Outside. In all kinds of weather. The only limit I had was daylight. Up north in the rain and darkness, the chances of me getting hit by a car were huge—even on the sidewalk. (I nearly got hit on the sidewalk dozens of times, in the bright light of day. Tourist town with distracted drivers. It was awful.)

The daylight thing meant that I would change my writing to post-exercise on the shortest days of the year which meant that winter became my least productive time, rather than most productive, as it had been for years. But, exercise before writing, remember. Those priorities. And damn if I didn't feel better after a run or a walk, even in the bracing cold.

I started running because of time. It takes me nearly two hours to get 10,000 steps. It takes me forty minutes if I'm going slowly to run three miles, which for me is 7,500 to 9,000 steps (depending on the path I use). I trained myself to run, even though I thought I would hate it, to get more writing time.

Turned out that after the pain of learning how to do it, I liked running better than any other exercise. Still do.

But running was a time saver. I had a lot of time savers built into my life, so that I could gain more hours of alertness for my writing.

I automated as many things as possible, setting times for all kinds of things. Laundry on down days (extra steps) because laundry takes no brain power. Meal planning and prep, with lots of big meals that would allow me to freeze food for those days when I didn't trust myself to cook. (That has changed here in Las Vegas, because I can get take-out or delivery if I'm having a really bad day.) And so on. Everything had its place in the schedule, based on how much brain power it took.

Top of the brain power list, of course, was fiction writing.

So many writing gurus advise that you set an hour count (work five to eight hours per day) or a word count. Which is well and good for the healthy folk, but for someone with a chronic illness, a daily quota is as impossible as a day job. I never know if I'm going to get gassed out by someone wearing too much cologne or if I'm going to accidentally walk into a store that reeks of incense because some idiot owner believes that's enticing to customers.

I have those issues less here, but when I lived up north, something as simple as stepping into a crowd might make me sick for days. Not to mention all those years when I didn't have the migraines firmly under control.

I had plans for work that I could do when I couldn't write fiction.

In fact, my alertness to-do list looks something like this:
Fully alert: Fiction
Slight headache/brain fog: nonfiction
Headache/brain fog: reading/editing
Bad headache/brain fog: TV or movie watching

Of course, if the headache/brain fog was so bad that I couldn't look at a screen, I would sleep. Sometimes that made things better. Often it made things worse.

I'm going to add how the exercise would fit into those categories now:
Fully alert: Fiction or exercise
Slight headache/brain fog: nonfiction or exercise
Headache/brain fog: exercise or reading/editing
Bad headache/brain fog: TV or movie watching

Note that I could exercise with a headache, but not with a bad headache. It was too dangerous. I wasn't alert enough to see a curb, let alone cross a street.

But I learned after I started walking and running outside that a walk in the bracing fresh air sometimes cleared up a headache or at least made it recede enough for me to work on nonfiction.

So exercise had its list as well.

The days in which I couldn't work at writing or editing at all became my days off. They were rest days, and if I actually *used* them to rest, I would be better quicker than if I worried about them or tried to force myself to work.

I gave myself permission to be sick, usually after trying to get some words or exercise under my belt. And that was how I lived for a long time.

So…I needed to maximize those alert hours.

I did so by having lists of projects, and what I would work on next. Again, the less time I spent dithering over what to do gave me more time to do whatever I needed to.

I broke my workday into segments:
1-2 hours writing.
Lunch
Exercise
1-2 hours writing
Dinner
Bonus time (maybe)

Or…in the winter
Exercise
Lunch
1-2 hours writing
Short break
1-2 hours writing
Dinner
Bonus time (maybe)

There were many days when I only got the one to two hours of writing done along with the exercise. And in the winter, those one to two hours were always a struggle.

I did my very best to get at least 1,000 words done no

matter how my headache was or how bad I felt. Even with a brain fog, I could manage a bit of nonfiction. I usually got more than 1,000 words done, because once I got started, I would keep going to the end of a scene. But 1,000 words was a small goal, and a doable one in less than an hour. I felt like I accomplished something.

A thousand words of new material five days per week is 5,000 words per week, or 260,000 words of new material per year. That's about three 90,000 word novels. Three novels is prolific by traditional publishing standards—hell, by any standards.

I usually wrote a lot more than that. In fact, I don't think I've ever had a year that low on word count because I would have 5,000 word days mixed with 3,000 word days mixed with the 1,000 word days.

The key was the two-part minimum: I had to try at least an hour of writing, and in that hour, try to get 1,000 words.

If I couldn't do either, fine. I would default to the other parts of my list.

But if I did, then that was a victory.

Victories are important. Because in a world where everyone else seems to have more energy and an ability to get more than one task done per day, it's so easy for a chronically ill person to see life as a series of failures.

I can't becomes more prevalent than *I can*.

Rather than set myself up for failure every day by trying to hit some artificial goal of a word count or hours at my desk, I had a vague goal to do 1,000 in an hour. If I didn't make it, I didn't beat myself up. I celebrated whenever I did make it, and marked those victories in my calendar.

When I was writing novels for traditional publishers, I set my deadlines (they ask you to) at a pace that was roughly equivalent to the one I listed above. I planned 5,000 words per week on a novel. I usually got much more than that. Either I turned the book in early or I worked on other projects at the same time.

And somehow, through all of that, I became known as prolific, even though I was struggling each and every day.

I think the biggest part of being productive for me, especially when I was really ill, was that I believed I could do the minimum every single day. A glance back in my calendar shows me that missing the minimum happened every week for me. But so did exceeding the minimum. And it all balanced out.

Priorities helped me choose what to do every day—family, health, writing. If something didn't fit in those categories, it came in lower on the priority list. Which made saying no to things easier, and allowed me to make choices that benefitted me.

My life is different now because I'm healthier. I can do more than one thing in a day. In fact, today I went to a meeting, went out to lunch, wrote 3,000 words and once I'm done with this, I'll head to the gym to do my daily run. (It's too cold and windy to run outside today.) Then I'll come back and read.

That's a normal person's life and unless someone at the gym is wearing too much cologne, I'll manage it.

But I recognize that this life is unusual for someone who suffers from a chronic illness. It was nearly impossible for me to have a day like this as recently as a year ago.

I feel fortunate that I can do it.

But I know how to remain productive if my health gets worse.

It's all about planning, priorities, and energy evaluation. And self-care. Always self-care.

Which is why I'm heading to the gym. Right now.

DISCIPLINE

FINISHED ON JUNE 2, 2009

I don't want to write this post. I have half a dozen reasons—some of them very good—as to why. First, my chronic illness has flared this week, so I'm struggling against my health. Second, Thursday is one of my annual days off, and I usually post the *Guide* (2019 note: *The Freelancer's Survival Guide* which is how my long-time blog started) on Thursday. If I were working a regular job, this day off would be on my calendar—and would have been since before I was hired. Third, I am moving my office and it looks like this week is D-Day for the desk, computer, printer, and calendar, the very things I use to write 95% of the time.

Those are the good reasons. Here are the whiney reasons: First, my office cat died two weeks ago. I really don't like going into my office when she's not there. Second, I gave up my nonfiction career for a reason twenty-three years ago. I don't like writing nonfiction. It's work. Fiction, on the other hand, is fun. Third, I've been doing this *Guide* for a while now and it's no longer new (or as my husband would say, it's not bright and shiny), so it's become a chore—something with a deadline that must be met, instead of something I look forward to doing.

I might admit the whiney reasons to friends. But here are the final reasons, the ones that come up when I'm tired and not feeling well, like today. First, I'd rather be reading. (Honestly, I'd always rather be reading.) Second, I want cake. (That's Thursday.) Third, I want to watch the news. And get e-mail. And go on Twitter. And surf the net. And, and, and…

I don't want to be sitting in my empty office, groggy from a nap that only left me feeling marginally better, writing part of a book that isn't under contract and might never be.

So why am I here?

Because I anticipated this day. Seriously. I knew this day was coming. And I planned for it.

Here's why I'm sitting in my empty office, groggy from a nap that left me feeling only marginally better, writing part of a book that isn't under contract.

You.

I have met my deadline on the *Freelancer's Guide* every week since April 2nd. I post, you make comments and e-mail me. Some of you have donated to the *Guide*, and some of you have subscribed, so I have a very real obligation to hit the mark, week after week, until this project is done.

That's the main reason. In fact, that's the only reason I'm here this week.

That reason negates all the complaints I had in the first paragraph.

But the complaints in the second—the ones I call the whiney reasons—have come up before. And despite the fact that two of them sound project-specific, they're not. They come up, with different rationales, with every single project I work on.

I would always rather start a new project than work through the middle of another project. And the *Freelancer's Guide* is in the muddy middle. How far into the middle, I can't tell you. I can never estimate easily how much material I have left.

Besides, I love beginnings. Not the actual moment of work, which can be hard as I try to figure out how to approach the project, but grooming the idea and preparing it for the actual writing. That bright and shiny part of writing is appealing to me, and I always have more than one project going just to keep that bright and shiny part of my brain occupied.

I work well at the end of a project as well. Gone are the days when I'd just skip the end. (I got tired of Dean looking at me and saying, "You skipped the last 10,000 words *again*.") When I know how something will end, I want it finished, and I work harder to get it done so that I can move onto the bright and shiny new thing.

Then there's the daily battle against "I want to read" and "I want to eat" and "I want to see a movie/news/TV." The battle against "I want to be doing something else, something that sounds fun, because right now, this project isn't fun."

Or as I usually say to someone who complains on television (and dammit, they can't hear me), "Wah."

Discipline gets a freelancer past all the complaints, but it's not the discipline you imagine from all those movies about military school or from watching Tiger Woods' (pre-divorce) interviews about his dogged determination to be the first on the course and the last to leave.

Discipline gets the job done, as Malcolm Gladwell noted in his controversial book, *Outliers*. The musicians who put in more practice hours have more success than those who put in fewer hours. Same with athletes, and same with writers and almost everyone else in the arts. Both Bill Clinton and Barack Obama spent more time on the campaign trail in their initial successful presidential bids than any of their opponents did—both in hours per day, and days per week.

But *how* did they do that? How do some musicians, playing the same instrument with the same intensity as other musicians, manage to hit the practice room more often? Why does Tiger Woods work harder than *every other professional golfer* on the course—especially since he says, quite frankly, that it's the hours of practice that make him the golfer he is.

Let's stick with Tiger for a moment. My husband used to be a professional golfer, so golf is important to our household, and Dean has more insight than most about the sport. We've watched Tiger since he won the U.S. Amateur competition in the 1990s. Dean told me then that this kid would be a phenom, and he is.

More than a decade later, Tiger Woods can rest on his laurels, but he doesn't. He won the U.S. Open in 2008, playing for four days with a destroyed knee and a cracked bone. Golf days last six hours or so, and golf, for those of you who don't play or follow the sport, hurts knees more than any other part of the body because of an unnatural twisting motion that the golfer must make when he swings.

It takes discipline to go to that course every day, in extreme pain, but you see it not just in Tiger Woods, but in most athletes at the pro level. It's so bad in most professional sports that teams have doctors on stand-by to order a badly injured player off the court/field so that the injury will not become permanent and career ending.

What causes this attitude? Sportscasters call that "heart," but it's more than heart. We've all seen high school players with heart, players who will give their all when the time comes to win the big game.

But it's not the big game that matters. It's the practice. It's sitting down to play scales for the 50,000th time because you need to warm up your hands before getting to Mozart. It's the drudgery of the same thing every day, with no defined ending.

It's the ability to overcome the urge to grab the bright and shiny and interesting to finish what you've started.

It's—and I'm sorry to say this, folks—it's what gets you to your day job five days per week, fifty-two weeks per year.

The problem is that most people don't apply that same discipline to their freelance work. There are reasons for this, which I'll get to. And, before the comments come in, let me add that I do realize that most people at a day job are not working at their best. Maybe they never do as well as they could. Many never reach their full potential. Most don't even try.

So what is it that makes some people work hard at their freelance careers while others work hard enough to get by or can't figure out a way to work at all?

It's not discipline. It's figuring out how to get yourself to work.

Seriously. What gets most people to their day jobs isn't the job. It's the money they get from the job, money that lets them pay the bills and support their families. Sure, a handful *like* their work, but most like the paycheck and benefits better.

Here's the problem: there are no paychecks and benefits when you work for yourself. If that's your motivation for working, then you're not going to have much luck freelancing —providing you carry that motivation into your freelance work.

Let's boil it down a bit more. When you begin freelancing, you do it for the love. Often you wait for the muse or until you get an order or if a friend asks for your help with something that you're good at. Eventually, you make some money at this, and then you realize you might be able to make a living at it.

Already bad habits have formed. You start doing this as a hobby, *after* everything else of importance gets finished. It feels natural to do the freelance work last.

Other things are always important. Your daughter skins her knee, the phone rings, a friend needs help moving. You have to learn to make your hobby or the thing you did only when you "had time" become your first priority.

How do you do that?

Unfortunately, I can't tell you. What you need to do is specific to you. There is no magic bullet, no one-size-fits-all answer.

But let me give you some ideas, based on my own experience.

And as I typed those words, I heard my writing friends giggle. They are all convinced that I'm the most disciplined person they know. They're wrong. In most things, I lack discipline entirely.

Unlike most of my writing friends, I have not held a full-time job for years. Why? Discipline. At some point, the paycheck isn't enough for me. I hate having someone tell me what to do, and that always triumphs.

Even the radio job which I loved didn't last long. I quit four separate times. Each time the station hired me to be *interim* news director at my insistence. I didn't want the permanent job. So I stayed until someone new came on board, and came back as interim director when that someone new left. I remained at the station in between *as a volunteer*, working a few nights per week. But I didn't want to be an employee there. The only thing that broke that years-long cycle, by the way, was my move out of town.

Discipline has always been a major issue for me. I get bored easily, and I don't play well with others. So hiring a personal trainer, for example, would never work for me. I would do my best to circumvent anything the trainer told me.

In my forties, I had a piano teacher. I stayed until I learned how to play the instrument adequately. Then I realized I was seeing how much practice it actually took to convince the teacher I had spent days at it instead of an hour or two. Once I fooled her a few times, we were done.

This is why I never became a musician. I didn't have the discipline. And I love music. At one point in my life, I played fifteen different instruments. (Only two of them really well.) I just don't love music enough to conquer my discipline problem.

I love writing enough to work through each issue as it comes up. How? By figuring out what stopped me from getting a day's worth of work.

Each time I solved one issue, another cropped up. Then I would have to solve that one. This pattern continues to this day.

When I discuss this with students, I tell them that gaining discipline is a series of mind games. Your mind will find good and effective ways to stop you. You have to figure out ways around them. The old cliché about when a door closes, go through a window applies here.

I can sense the frustration among you now. I'm not being specific enough to help. So let's go back through my initial points, above, and I'll tell you how I get around them. Maybe that will strike a chord.

First, health issues. I imagine making my excuses to a boss. If a good boss would let me go home sick or encourage me to stay away from the office, then I stay away from the computer. But if I can put in a day of so-so work, I do. I store up projects for days when my illness is present, but not so bad that I have to spend the day in bed. Those are the projects I do when I'm not feeling well.

Second, my annual days off. I have a few of them—birthday, anniversary, Christmas, and a couple of others. If I don't take those days, I'm angry at myself. Sometimes I take an entire week around it. That's just reasonable for any job.

Third, moving my office. I haven't done that for years. It's a good excuse not to work, except that I have deadlines, just like you would at a day job. I had to figure out a way to work while I'm in the middle of this transition. Because if it's not this transition, it's another transition. Life is full of them, and you have to figure out how to put in your freelance hours, even while everything changes around you.

But those are bigger events. It's the small ones that interfere with discipline. Let's address what I call the whiney complaints.

First, I would rather read. It took me an entire summer to figure out that reading, for me, will suck all my time out of every single day. I cannot start a book with breakfast or I will read until I go to bed.

How did I discover this? I had a day job that went part-time. I opted to take the afternoons off. When the job had been full-time, I read during my lunch break. So I continued this habit on the part-time schedule—and got nothing done.

I tried "disciplining" myself. I would put the book down and try to go to work, only to find myself reading again. "Disciplining"—forcing myself to quit—didn't work. No matter how hard I tried, I simply could not stop reading, even when I finished the book. I'd move to the next one.

So the key for me wasn't *quitting* reading. It was *not starting*. I set the books aside until I got x-amount of work done each day.

This isn't easy. It required actual hiding of the books. I enlisted my then-husband's help, making sure the books were out of sight.

Eventually, I learned that I worked hard and fast if I knew I could read when I was done. I got my work done, and then I read. Problem solved.

It sounds so easy, but it took months of trial and error. No amount of "forcing" myself got me to change my habits. I had to figure out where the problem started, and nip it in the bud.

Second, I want cake. (Don't we all?) That's usually a sign to me that I'm hungry. I need to figure out if I'm really hungry or —catch this—bored with what I'm doing. If I'm bored, I think I'm hungry, because that's one of the few things I will get up from my desk to deal with. If I need a meal, I eat. But my subconscious loves to trick me (and my hips) by convincing me to leave when I'm not through.

Often, the "I'm hungry" reaction comes when I'm working on something particularly difficult or something I don't want to do. Again, it took many months (and too many calories) to figure this one out. Now, before I get something to eat, I ask myself this: Do I like what I'm working on? If the answer is no, I generally stay at my desk.

Note that I do not ask myself if I'm hungry. I've already identified hungry, and the answer would be yes. But I figured out that my subconscious has learned a mind game to convince me to get away from the computer, one that makes me think I'm hungry (or craving food, like cake) and gets me to leave *when I don't need to.*

We all have mind games like this, and they're hard to identify. The question should always be: Is work going well? Because if it is, and I'm hungry, I have trouble tearing myself away. If it isn't, I'll make up any damn reason to leave my desk.

Third, I want to watch the news, download e-mail, look at the internet, do Twitter…in other words, do something else entirely.

This was almost as bad for me as reading was. I learned to keep my office spare. My computer has internet access and it also has e-mail access. I have shut those programs down. I've tossed away all games that were initially on my computer. There is no phone or television in my office. I have a stereo and a radio turned to a classical channel. No news of any kind allowed here.

Why? Because they all distract me. Rather than "discipline" myself to overcome the temptation, I remove the temptation entirely. In order to download my e-mail, I have to go to a different computer, one with an existing e-mail program, and download from there. I need to go to a different room to watch television. I can't even hear the phone ring in my office.

These were all tough things to learn. The internet is particularly sneaky because you feel like you're working when you're online. You are not working—even if, like me, a small part of your business comes through the internet. You're not doing your core business. I have a number of writing friends who refuse to remove the internet from their computers. Those friends get very little done. All of them have spouses who work, and so the writer doesn't have to bring in a lot of money. All of them frown at me when I suggest removing the internet from their writing computers.

Everyone has these leaks, as the poker players call it. A leak is something that drains your income, something that has nothing to do with your work. And it's often something you're not willing to give up.

You have to learn how to control this leak and make it work for you. And, here's the tough part: If you can't control it, seek help. I went into therapy a number of years ago to help with one of my writing issues, something that got in the way of my business. And much as I hate authority, I listened to that counselor, because being a successful writer meant more to me than the leak.

However, had we worked on my discipline issues with music, I probably would have blown off the therapy within weeks. I have never had the discipline there, and I really don't want it. Not deep down.

And that's the final issue. If you want a successful freelance career of any kind, you'll overcome the things that get in your way. You can't do it all at once. You have to tackle one problem at a time. But you're willing to work on those problems.

If you're not willing to solve the problem after years of trying, then you probably don't want this freelance career (whatever it is) as much as you think you do.

Discipline is not about forcing yourself to improve. It's about wanting to get better.

That's the difference between Tiger Woods and all those other golfers. Tiger wants to be the best, and he knows the only way to do that is to work harder than everyone else. But he doesn't define himself as the best *right now*. He means *the best ever*. He keeps Jack Nicklaus's stats on his wall, trying to beat them. Tiger's not playing the current field. He's playing the entire field from the dawn of recorded golf history.

And he's doing a good job at knocking down the records.

But here's the key. He's not doing this for his fans. He's not doing it for his (late) father or for golf history. He's doing it for himself. Because he wants to. Because that's his goal.

So...

How do you get disciplined?

Here are a few thoughts.

. . .

1. Define what you want to achieve.

Not other people's goals for you. Not what your parents want or your spouse wants. What do you want? And how badly to do you want it? Will you die disappointed if you don't achieve it? Will you feel like a failure? Or will you shrug and move onto the next thing?

2. Make a list of the things that get in the way of that achievement.

If everything you list comes from the outside, then you have another problem. For example, writers often say they can't get published because the publishing industry is impossible to crack or they need an agent or they can't figure out how to submit their work. Those, my friends, are excuses. Other people have succeeded in your industry. Figure out how they did it, and then try it yourself.

By "what gets in the way," I mean what part of *you* gets in the way. What are you doing to block your success? How do you change that? Sometimes the change is minor, like asking yourself whether you are really hungry or you are avoiding work. Sometimes the change is major, like the one thing I mentioned (deliberately vaguely) that forced me to go to therapy. I couldn't change that one on my own—but it was *my* problem, and I had to find a solution. I just needed help doing so.

3. Change your thought patterns.

When you decide to go full-time freelance, realize that your hobby has just become your job. That realization alone will take time. Then figure out how to make your freelance work a priority in your own mind. Apply patterns from your day job to your freelance work.

    Ask these questions:
        What made you go to your day job every morning?
        What made you stay there?
        What made you work on days when you felt crummy?
        What made you work on days when you had somewhere better to go?

And so on. Use those answers to design your freelance work.

For example, my husband Dean works hard when he's under deadline. He has trouble working when he has no deadlines at all. The key for him is to create deadlines—or to get someone from the outside (an editor, usually) to give him a deadline.

I didn't think I had that issue until I started the *Freelancer's Guide*. Then I realized that I never finish nonfiction unless I have a deadline. I don't like writing nonfiction. I love writing fiction and will do it without a deadline. But the deadline gets me to finish nonfiction projects—my two columns, some articles, and now this.

By meeting my deadline on this *Guide* every week, I've also established something else. I've got a streak going. I hate breaking streaks, so that's motivation to work on weeks like this one, when I could just as easily post a note that the *Guide* is on a one-week hiatus.

I learned long ago that I have to love what I'm doing to sustain the work. I loved working at the radio station, but hated it when I was in charge. So I kept quitting the paying work to go back to volunteering.

I love writing fiction, so I continue to do it, even when times are tough.

When I need to be disciplined, I have to find the love at the center of what I'm doing. Here's an example. I have tried to maintain a regular exercise program since middle-aged spread hit in my mid-thirties (thanks in part to that hunger thing, above).

I started with an exercise I love, swimming. But it was inconvenient. I had to drive half an hour each way to the pool. The hours were irregular, and I'd often lose too much work time. So I started riding my bicycle. I enlisted the help of a friend from the gym. I had to meet her at a designated time every day. That got me out of the house.

We couldn't sustain the rides. Then I fell off the bike and broke my arm, the second serious bike accident in my life. (The first, when I was nine, smashed my face so badly, I still have occasional dental surgeries to repair the damage.) I realized that cycling on the Oregon Coast along a highway with no bike lanes (there are none for more than 100 miles) is too dangerous for me.

So I decided to run. When I made this decision, I couldn't run for a minute without feeling ill. I didn't like it. I had never liked running. Worse, I got bored quickly.

But I love music. If a song that I like comes on the radio, I crank the volume. If I'm alone in the house, I dance. So I put my favorite CDs on my iPod, and promised myself I could run for the length of one song.

I couldn't, not for weeks. Eventually I managed. But I wasn't running because I liked running. I was using that time as an excuse to listen to my favorite music all by myself.

Two years later, I can run for 30 minutes straight. When I feel like it's time to find a new form of exercise, I realize it's time to change the music in my iPod. I'm bored with what's there. I would rather swim, honestly. I would like to be on my bike. But running works for me now. And I've become so conditioned to it that last week, when my iPod battery died, I played some music in my head and finished the workout.

Could I do that every time? Hell, no. But I know how to make myself go out for a daily run now—and how to enjoy it. Set the iPod on shuffle and see what songs come up.

It took me fifteen years to find a form of exercise I can do every day, rain or shine, one that I *will* do. And what gets me out there now isn't the exercise or the need for it.

It's the half an hour of music. Which I love.

So the most important aspect of discipline isn't discipline at all. It's this:

4. Find the love.

Find what you love about what you do, and channel that each and every day. Acknowledge it too. When I finish a run, I check in with myself. Inevitably, I feel better when I quit than I did when I started. I've told Dean that, and sometimes he's gotten me outside by reminding me of it. (I have to tell you, it sometimes pisses me off that I feel better *after* a run when I felt so crummy before the run.) Celebrate your achievement, even if that achievement is just getting to your desk.

Celebrate with something you enjoy.

I used to celebrate a day's writing by reading. Then I started editing, and reading ceased to be a reward for several years. In those years, I celebrated with a good movie or a guilty-pleasure TV show. Now I'm back to celebrating with reading.

Which is what I'm going to do now.

Oh, by the way, I'm no longer groggy from the nap, although I still feel under par. I did run today, and felt better afterwards (dammit!). And I got this section of the *Guide* done, two days early. I'll post it late tomorrow, which will be one day early. Then I'll get my day off. With cake.

That's my reward, along with all the fun things planned for that day.

And that was more than enough to get me into my chair today—even though I didn't want to be here.

CALLING IN SICK
FINISHED APRIL 14, 2009

How do you know when you're too sick to work? Seems easy enough to figure out, right? We're all adults. We know when we're sick. But for freelancers, that's a tougher question than it seems.

As I mentioned in the introduction (to *The Freelancer's Survival Guide*, which is where this first appeared), I suffer from a chronic illness. It reared its ugly head over the weekend. No one had sent me a question for this week, so I figured I'd use my own life experience to write this week's post.

We all get sick. The serious things—pneumonia, bronchitis, certain types of flu—leave us too ill to get out of bed. They're not the problem to the freelancer. The milder illnesses are.

When you work for someone else, it's easy to know when to go into work. If you had one of those cushy jobs with paid sick leave and paid vacation, chances are you took more sick days than you needed. If you were feeling a little off, and you had the paid time coming to you, you took the day and stayed home. Even seasonal allergies might have warranted a little paid "me" time.

If you had a by-the-hour job without those benefits, you took as little time off as possible. At my last waitressing job, the boss actually had rules about when *not* to come to work. (If you're contagious, she'd say, you must stay home.) People who work by the hour usually need the money. They come to work when they can barely walk because they don't dare lose the hours.

Freelancing is closer to the by-the-hour job, but it's not quite the same. When you freelance, you get paid for piecework. In other words, the more things you finish, the more you get paid.

You finish more things if you put in more hours.

Seems obvious, right? But most people aren't used to being their own boss. Most people are too lenient. They lose entire days to headaches or the sniffles because they're not feeling "up to par." Days, even weeks, go by while the freelancer waits to feel better.

Here's an ugly truth: *When you work at home, you have no colleagues to distract you. You're constantly assessing how you feel, and always coming up short.*

That's right. You'll probably feel worse day-to-day when you work at home. Some of it is the solitude. Some of it is the lack of exercise. Some of it is the lack of fresh air.

When you go to a job away from home, you have to walk outside and drive somewhere. When I started freelancing, I'd stay in the house for days on end. It took me a while to realize that a walk around the block was often enough to make me feel energetic and healthy.

So…how *do* you know if you're too sick to work?

It's simple. Imagine the toughest boss you ever worked for. Then imagine telling him (and my toughest boss was a man) that you can't come into work today because…and fill in the reason here.

If you can't imagine yourself telling Tough Boss that reason, then you go to work.

It goes like this: Hi, Tough Boss. I can't come to work today because I have a temperature of 102 and I'm heading to the doctor this afternoon.

Fine, good. My old Tough Boss would have let me out for that.

But imagine this one: Hi, Tough Boss. I can't come to work today because I'm feeling sluggish.

Or...

Hi, Tough Boss. I can't come to work today because I didn't get a good night's sleep last night.

Or...

Hi, Tough Boss. I can't come to work today because I'm not thinking as clearly as I usually do.

One or two of those with the Tough Boss I'd had (back in 1980—this dude really lives in my memory) and I would've been fired. Fast.

A friend once told me that people who work at corporate jobs aren't productive every moment of every day. They talk to their colleagues on company time. They daydream. They do make-work to look busy. This friend was a corporate manager who estimated that a good 40% of the time, his employees weren't working at their peak.

On the days they came in feeling "sluggish" or "tired," they probably got less done.

When you work for someone else, you get used to days like that. You know you won't get fired (unless you have other problems with job performance). Your employer knew that was part of the deal when he decided to hire employees in his business. Every self-employed person knows that the hardest worker in the company is always the boss.

On those days when you would go in to work with a mild

cold or allergies, you get what you could done. Sometimes, you got brownie points just for showing up and keeping your desk warm.

I was so used to working for myself that when I got my single full-time job back in 1984, I caused a huge stir in the office. I worked as an editorial assistant in a textbook publishing house. I got my day's assignments and usually finished them within the first hour of my eight-hour shift.

The other editorial assistants pulled me aside after a week of that and told me to slow down because I was making them look bad. I didn't get it. I figured I was there to *work*, so I worked. I could have done the work of all the editorial assistants and filled up my day. But that wasn't the corporate structure. So I did my hour's worth of work, and spent the remaining seven hours reading the books the company published. My boss promised to promote me if someone in editorial quit. Which no one had for nearly two years. After four months of that, I left the job because I was horribly, unbelievably bored.

(Years later, I got a great part-time job as a secretary for a forensic psychologist. He looked at my resume and said, "My biggest concern about you is that you're used to working for yourself. I'm hiring you to sit and answer phones. I'm afraid you might get bored." I told him about my experience at the textbook publisher and we both laughed about it. Then he agreed that I could write or read at my desk when he had nothing for me to do. Needless to say, that was the best job I ever had.)

If you had one of those jobs that let you slack off with regularity, then freelancing is going to be a big shock for you. Unless you modify your behavior right now, you'll be one of those freelancers who get nothing done for days on end, especially in spring allergy season or when the baby keeps you up all night.

No matter how dedicated you are, the reality is that there will be days when you feel sick, but not sick enough to stay home (from that imaginary Tough Boss). How do you do your best work when that happens?

Well, you don't. You figure out what tasks you can do. I'm writing this piece two days earlier than I planned because today, I'm surviving on Advil and caffeine.

I'm not thinking clearly enough to write fiction. So I'm doing tasks that I find easier than fiction writing. And yes, writing nonfiction is easier than fiction, at least for me. (Besides, I can always clean this essay up later if I don't like what I've done.)

I've been feeling punk for three days now. I've photocopied contracts, put together files for a project that I'm working on with a publisher in Virginia, did research on the next story I'm writing, and cleaned up my office.

I know the pattern of my chronic condition, so I know that in a day or two, I'll be back up to my normal level of energy. Why waste my good days on tasks I can do when I'm not feeling up to par? I'm planning ahead by doing some of this work before it's due.

This is exactly what you would have done at your day job if you were feeling a little under the weather, but you still managed to show up. You'd have done the things you'd been putting off, things that required less effort than your daily tasks.

Just think of Tough Boss. Make your excuses out loud, and see if they'll fly with him. If they won't, then go to your office. Do what you can.

You'll be happy that you did.

HEALTHY TIME OFF
FINISHED ON FEBRUARY 18, 2019

Well, here's a learning curve, one I hadn't expected. As my health returned and improved here in Las Vegas, I would get exhausted. I mean deeply and profoundly exhausted.

Dean laughed at me the first few times it happened, and he would say, "When was the last time you took time off?"

I would look at my calendars, where I record all the details of my life, from my steps to my exercise to my writing to my reading, and a few other miscellaneous things. And after some calendar study, I would realize that I had been going full-bore for at least two weeks before a collapse.

What's full-bore? At least 3,000 words per day. Twelve thousand steps (I upped my game on steps in 2016). Either a three-mile run or yoga or swimming or some other cross training. Daily time with Dean. Walking to lunch, movies, time with friends who were visiting. Always eight hours of sleep (or an attempt at it), but no more rest than that.

And lo and behold, I would get tired after about fourteen days of that. Who knew?

Normal people, apparently. People who don't have chronic health issues.

Those people take time off. Apparently, that's why the eight-hour workday exists, and why most employers give their people at least two days off.

Now, I realize that many, many, many people don't have the luxury of any time off. They work more than one job so they can make ends meet. Or they have children and spend the hours they're not working taking care of the kids. People with very young children rarely (never?) get eight hours of sleep.

But the fortunate ones, the ones who have good jobs and good health, the ones who have a spouse or family who help with child care, they have the luxury of real time off. And it makes them more alert. It makes them stronger. It makes them fresher during the week ahead.

And it prevents burnout, which science has shown over and over and over again.

Okay. I know all this stuff. But I never had to apply it to myself before. Because I wanted to get my writing done during those years when I was so very sick almost every day. So the days when I was really, really, really sick doubled as time off.

Yeah, I get it now.

I multitasked rest.

Who knew? (Beside my husband.)

This being healthy most of the time is still new to me. It hasn't even been a year yet. And I honestly don't know how to schedule the healthy time off yet because I have another problem.

I love writing and reading and (surprisingly to me) running. When I had a real day job, I wrote and read on my time off. Now, writing and reading are my day job, so what do I do on my time off?

I don't write on those days. I do read, but not for work.

(Reading is like breathing to me.) Because I now live in a city *and* I have money (not something I had the last time I lived in a city), I see a lot of theater and concerts. Sometimes I take the whole day off, sometimes just the evening. But those things revitalize me.

I'm also spending more time with friends. Because we're still new to town, we don't have a lot of local friends, although I'm slowly gathering some. But because we live in Las Vegas, we have friends visit from other places every month. So, we're getting a lot of socializing in, which is wonderful.

All of that is not-working. And that's helpful.

I also found that, for me, an evening out away from my desk or from thinking about writing or working is as good as a full day off.

I have no magic bullet on this one, because I'm still learning.

But those of you whose chronic illness comes and goes, or who have learned how to manage the illness as I have, need to pay attention to this. With some illnesses, exhaustion can bring the symptoms back, so learning how to rest *while healthy* is a complete necessity.

I had no idea. Really. Apparently, healthy also includes ups and downs. (It looked from the outside like healthy people could do anything.) The key is to maintain the joy in being healthy while making sure you're still doing self-care.

And one of the biggest parts of self-care is rest. A day per week, two days per week, whatever works for you.

I'm still figuring out what works for me. So that's why this chapter is a short heads-up rather than a "how I do it."

COMPARISONS
FINISHED ON FEBRUARY 19, 2019

When Dean and I first got together, we had a long discussion about careers. We were both new writers at the beginning of our careers. And we knew that our careers would not end up being the same. We had a long series of conversations about what we would do when one career was ascendant over the other.

Good thing, too. I won the John W. Campbell Award for Best New Writer shortly after we got together. For about ten years, I was on all the award ballots. Dean's books sold more copies, but I got more attention.

Right now, he's the one who is getting attention. He has done videos that have gone viral. His Cold Poker Gang series sells like crazy.

If we hadn't been aware of the potential differences in our careers from the very start, we probably would not have been together for more than thirty years.

Comparison is a natural thing. It's how we learn. Watch toddlers sometimes. They mirror their parents, sometimes literally— trying to sit like Daddy or moving their hands (or trying to) the way that Mommy is. We look to others to see what's possible.

It's hard to stop doing that, particularly when we're only seeing others from the outside. It still surprises me when I hear very successful people talk about their struggles. The skier Lindsey Vonn has been upfront about her injuries and her goals, how she managed her profession day to day while dealing with so much pain that I can't quite imagine it. Yet to look at her, pretty, blond, smart, and athletic, without knowing any of that, you'd think her life is perfect.

Writers are even more mysterious than celebrities. You see their output, but not their daily struggles to get it done. Everyone puts a good face on what they're doing, particularly on social media. Sure, a handful of people log onto their accounts and outline how depressing their day is, but most only talk about the highlights.

I'm as guilty of that as the next person. I don't like sharing the bad things. I love sharing the good.

But the struggles? They're personal. Not to mention the fact that I'm not the most touchy-feely person. I would prefer to discuss books than health problems—mine or anyone else's.

That makes comparisons even tougher.

As I've said repeatedly in this book, I'm considered prolific. So from the outside, I look like a writing machine to many writers. I've heard that over and over again: How I'm so dedicated and strong and am all about writing.

It doesn't feel that way from the inside. I don't write nearly enough. I never get to everything I want to do. I feel like I'm doing things other than writing most of the time.

It's even harder considering that I live with an extremely healthy former professional athlete. Dean, even as he ages, gets more done in a single day than some people do in six months. If he sets a goal of 10,000 words per day, he hits that goal. He doesn't have to stop because he got brain fog or needs extra sleep.

He did suffer from severe migraines when I met him, and that did slow him down, but he had such a healthy base that he could do amazing things on the days he wasn't down with a headache. I never had that healthy base.

If I compare my daily word count to his, I always fall short. He can be much more consistent than I am and he can write more. He's a sprint writer, though, so he often stops to do something else. I wish he wouldn't, because I love his work and want more of it, but I understand.

I suspect the sprint writing is his way of resting. He goes hard and then takes time off, just like the running guides tell you to do when you're in training for a sporting event. You work hard, then you taper. You do the event, and rest afterwards before starting hard training again.

That's his history as an athlete and he took it to writing.

I couldn't do athletic things as a younger person, so I learned how to write around illness, rather than the other way around.

The comparisons end here, though, because they're not useful. No matter how hard I try, I can't do things the way he can. And no matter how hard he tries, he has been unable to break the start/stop sprint aspect of his career (careers). That's his work method.

Most writers aren't lucky enough to live with another writer. They don't get into the nitty-gritty of someone else's routine. Most writers have the Imagined Routine of Favorite Writer or Role Model and then their own routine. And their routine never measures up to the imagined routine.

So rather than let the comparisons overwhelm, try this.

Celebrate your achievements.

Dean actually taught me that early in our relationship. I

have since learned it's another sports thing. Once I started running five days per week, I realized that all runs are not created equal. Some are great; some suck. And getting to the run isn't easy either. Some days, that's all I want to do. Mostly, though, the running, like my steps, is a serious inconvenience. I would so much rather sit on my butt and write and read or go to a movie or go out for a meal or spend time with Dean.

But all the running guides point this out: if you go out for ten minutes (even if your normal is an hour), count that as a victory, especially on the tough days.

Here's the secret: if you go out for ten minutes, you often do your usual run.

That was a great rule of thumb for me with the running because it got me out, even on rainy days (up north) and on days with the beginnings of a migraine. On the rainy days, I'd often have the most fun, because running in the rain makes me feel like a little kid. I actually run and laugh. (Even here: I did a 5K in February and it rained, and I found such joy in getting wet.)

However, with the headache, I was never certain if I could run until I tried. Sometimes I'd run for ten minutes, and the headache would get significantly worse. A few times, up north, I'd start the run and realize I would have trouble making it home. On those days, I'd run toward the WMG offices, which were a mile from my house. I could always get to WMG and catch a ride home.

That sounds like a defeat, doesn't it? My run ended because of my headache.

But I never saw it that way. I would get a half mile of running, usually, and some walking, as well as some fresh air. Considering how ill I was, that was a victory.

A major victory.

I learned to apply that attitude to my writing as well. If I was really sick, and I managed to get 500 words on a day when I could barely crawl out of bed, then that was a victory. It wasn't a qualified victory. It was a real victory.

What do I mean by a qualified victory?

I mean this: *Considering how sick I was, that was pretty good.*

No. Get rid of the qualifier. How many other people could get 500 words in a day *while healthy*? How many other people have the determination to write at all?

Five hundred words that day was great. It was amazing. And I pat myself on the back for getting that much done.

Sometimes I pat myself on the back for the planning. Yesterday, for instance. I had a busy day. I had a yoga class in the morning, and Dean and I had some planned time off in the afternoon—going to see a movie. We also planned our steps at the local mall, to do some browsing.

But I want to finish this book, and I had a hunch I'd be too tired when I got home. (Turned out, I had a migraine from some perfume. Which I found ironic, given that I'm working on this book.) Since I knew I'd be busy, I got up early enough to write one of the chapters before I went to yoga.

And sure enough, that was all the writing I managed yesterday. But I was and am happy with that. I planned well, and that's a victory.

A friend of mine has a saying about certain people. He says that they can find the dark cloud in any silver lining.

In other words, they can make any positive experience negative.

I sure get that. It's really easy for those of us who suffer from a chronic illness to beat ourselves up for all of our body's failings. In fact, that's often the default for us. It's about what we *can't* do rather than what we *can* do.

I'm as guilty as anyone else of that.

But mostly, I try as hard as I can to savor the silver linings. And the rainbows. And the sunshine.

I like to see accomplishing things—even small things—as victories. The more victories I have, the more victories I want.

And that keeps me going, even on the hard days.

So stop comparing yourself to some imagined ideal. Start celebrating what you accomplish. Make a list of your daily victories.

You'll be surprised, over the space of a year, just how much you'll accomplish.

And how much fun you'll have doing it.

THE POINT
FINISHED ON FEBRUARY 19, 2019

What's the point?

I can't tell you how many times writers ask me that question. What's the point of all the struggle? Why am I even trying? Who cares that I write? No one buys my books anyway.

(Note that writers of all levels say that last sentence, because they compare. No one buys the book might mean it sells no copies at all or it might mean that "only" 100 people bought copies or that the book isn't selling millions of copies. Again, the evils of comparison.)

So…what is the point?

Aside from doing something you love, which shouldn't be an aside at all?

The point is your perspective.

You are a unique individual with a unique point of view. No one else views the world the way that you do. No one else could.

Sure, there are seven plots and Shakespeare wrote them all better, as one of my creative writing instructors once said. So what? Shakespeare is dead, and you're not.

The only way that some of us will experience your perspective is if you write it down. If you write one of those seven plots from your point of view, rather than some old dead playwright's. You might never know that the person who loves your work so much they reread it dozens of times. But that person is out there. You just have to write and put the work out there—whatever that means for you.

It'll take time to find your reader. Or rather, for your reader to find you. And you might never know who they are. But keep writing. Keep struggling. Keep *enjoying*.

Because the more fun you have writing, the more fun they'll have reading. Even if you're writing about your struggles. *Especially* if you're writing about your struggles.

We all struggle in our own ways. We have our own goals and desires, successes and failures. And we learn from each other, if we only talk about those things.

That's the lesson I'm taking from planning this book. I hadn't realized how silent I had been. I'm still going to be reticent; that's my way. But I'm struggling, just like you are.

And I'm enjoying.

Writing is the highlight of my day. Every day. I wouldn't work so hard to get to the keyboard if writing wasn't the highlight.

I hope it's your highlight as well. I hope you enjoy writing. And I hope it brings you great joy.

Good luck with your struggles. Celebrate your victories. And have fun.

That's the point.

I value honest feedback, and would love to hear your opinion in a review, if you're so inclined, on your favorite book retailer's site.

Be the first to know!

Please sign up for the Kristine Kathryn Rusch newsletter, and receive exclusive content, keep up with the latest news, releases and so much more—even the occasional giveaway.

So, what are you waiting for? To sign up go to kristinekathrynrusch.com.

But wait! There's more. Sign up for the WMG Publishing newsletter, too, and get the latest news and releases from all of the WMG authors and lines, including Kristine Grayson, Kris Nelscott, Dean Wesley Smith, *Fiction River: An Original Anthology Magazine, Smith's Monthly,* and so much more.

To sign up go to wmgpublishing.com.

For writers, discoverability means the difference between gaining an audience and publishing into the void. *New York Times* bestselling author Kristine Kathryn Rusch deftly tackles the topic in this latest WMG Writers' Guide.

> "Kristine [Kathryn Rusch]'s extensive experience in both traditional and indie publishing shines through in this amazing book."
>
> — Tim Grahl, "11 Best Book Marketing Books"

> "There are lots of books out there about how to market your book. Some of them are good. Some aren't. *Discoverability* is one of the best…"
>
> — TeleRead

"Kristine Kathryn Rusch's new book *Discoverability* is by far the best resource I have read to date to help indie authors succeed after the book is written."

— Chris Syme, Principal of CKSyme Media Group

ABOUT THE AUTHOR

New York Times bestselling author Kristine Kathryn Rusch writes in almost every genre. Generally, she uses her real name (Rusch) for most of her writing. Under that name, she publishes bestselling science fiction and fantasy, award-winning mysteries, acclaimed mainstream fiction, controversial nonfiction, and the occasional romance. Her novels have made bestseller lists around the world and her short fiction has appeared in eighteen best of the year collections. She has won more than twenty-five awards for her fiction, including the Hugo, *Le Prix Imaginales*, the *Asimov's* Readers Choice award, and the *Ellery Queen Mystery Magazine* Readers Choice Award.

Publications from *The Chicago Tribune* to *Booklist* have included her Kris Nelscott mystery novels in their top-ten-best mystery novels of the year. The Nelscott books have received nominations for almost every award in the mystery field, including the best novel Edgar Award, and the Shamus Award.

She writes goofy romance novels as award-winner Kristine Grayson.

She also edits. Beginning with work at the innovative publishing company, Pulphouse, followed by her award-winning tenure at *The Magazine of Fantasy & Science Fiction*, she took fifteen years off before returning to editing with the original anthology series *Fiction River*, published by WMG Publishing. She acts as series editor with her husband, writer Dean

Wesley Smith, and edits at least two anthologies in the series per year on her own.

To keep up with everything she does, go to kriswrites.com and sign up for her newsletter. To track her many pen names and series, see their individual websites (krisnelscott.com, kristinegrayson.com, retrievalartist.com, divingintothewreck.com).

Keep informed:
www.kriswrites.com

Made in the USA
San Bernardino, CA
15 September 2019